S.P. Taylor-Helps

GW00566954

INTO THIN AIR
People Who Disappear

PAUL BEGG

DAVID & CHARLES
Newton Abbot London North Pomfret (Vt)

British Library Cataloguing in Publication Data

Begg, Paul
   Into Thin Air
   1. Missing persons
   I. Title
   001.9'4   HV6762.A3

   ISBN 0–7153–7724–8

First published March 1979
Second impression May 1979

Printed in Great Britain
by Redwood Burn Limited, Trowbridge & Esher
for David & Charles (Publishers) Limited
Brunel House Newton Abbot Devon

Published in the United States of America
by David & Charles Inc
North Pomfret Vermont 05053 USA

Contents

In memory of my father and Timmy.
For my Mother, Jim, and especially Judy,
without whom, to quote that hackneyed phrase,
this book would never have been written.

Part One: Disappearances on Land

1 Missing Persons

'Relatives are anxious to trace' . . . 'missing from home' . . .
'last seen wearing' . . . 'described as being' . . .

Nobody knows how many people disappear every year.
Conservative estimates are disturbingly high, suggesting that in
the UK alone between 11,000 and 26,000 people 'go missing'
annually. The majority of these people are found, but some
never are: they seem to have vanished from the face of the
Earth, and for no apparent reason.

The London Metropolitan Police receive about 20,000
missing-person reports every year (about 55 a day). Most of
these missing people are found, often within a few hours of
the report being filed, but those who are still missing after a
period of forty-eight hours are listed with full particulars on
the Missing Persons Register, which also includes details of
all missing persons registered at the request of provincial and
overseas forces. In 1977 the Metropolitan Police Missing
Persons Register contained the names and particulars of 4,715
people:

METROPOLITAN POLICE MISSING PERSON STATISTICS

	1975	1976	1977
Total number of missing persons placed on the register at New Scotland Yard	4,953	4,891	6,096
Total number of missing persons placed on the register at the request of provincial and overseas forces	1,234	1,322	2,022
Total number of missing persons in the Metropolitan Police District, excluding those placed on the register at the request of other forces	3,719	3,569	4,074

BREAKDOWN OF METROPOLITAN POLICE CASES

	1975	1976	1977
Boys under 14 years of age	321	296	328
Girls under 14 years of age	327	264	332
Boys between 14 and 17 years	766	743	764
Girls between 14 and 17 years	1,471	1,474	1,660
Men	452	391	505
Women	382	401	485
TOTAL	3,719	3,569	4,074

STILL MISSING AT THE END OF THE YEAR

Boys under 14 years of age	35	50	17
Girls under 14 years of age	36	26	26
Boys between 14 and 17 years	79	87	43
Girls between 14 and 17 years	166	166	133
Men	60	65	94
Women	45	55	65
TOTAL	421	449	378

Only 378 out of over 4,000 reported missing persons were unaccounted for at the end of 1977, so the police obviously do a remarkable job of tracking down runaways. Nevertheless, 378 is a very disturbing figure, suggesting that perhaps as many as 7 people disappear every week – and this only from London!

It is not an offence to disappear, and the police are not obliged to launch an investigation unless the missing person is subject to a Probation Order or a similar directive requiring that he or she live in a certain place, or is under 18 years of age, in which case the Children and Young Persons Act (1969) demands that the police investigate and ensure that the juvenile is safe and in satisfactory surroundings. However, the police do investigate most cases, particularly if a crime is suspected, or if the missing person is known to have been depressed or suicidal, or if there is obvious cause for concern due to age or illness; they do not investigate if the missing person is believed to have 'gone missing' of his or her own accord.

Once an investigation has been launched, the police are unceasing in their efforts to trace a missing person and in some cases the particulars of the missing person are circulated to every police force in the country. No name is removed from the register until the person has been found and every line of inquiry is followed up, but investigations often have a sad or inglorious end when the missing persons are found dead or, if alive, protesting against what they see as an invasion of privacy. Moreover, the police cannot inform anxious relatives of a missing person's whereabouts without the runaway's permission.

By far the largest proportion of missing people are juveniles, the majority being girls under the age of 18 years. Children disappear for several reasons, although the most common cause is an attempt to escape alleged parental domination – which explains why more girls than boys vanish: they reach puberty earlier and thus become restless at an earlier age.

Juveniles are the most difficult of all runaways to find. They are not as well documented as adults nor as fixed in their habits, and they generally head for the bright lights and 'golden pavements' of the big cities, where they often sink into the sordid world of pimps, prostitutes and pornography dealers, all of whom have a market for kids.

The grotesque Dickensian underworld which still flourishes in London (and most major cities), complete with latter-day Fagins and Artful Dodgers, was revealed to British television audiences on Tuesday, 22 July 1975, when a documentary called *Johnny Go Home* was broadcast. (The British Academy of Film and Television Arts subsequently voted it the best factual programme of the year.) *Johnny Go Home* came into being when the authors of the programme literally tripped over a couple of children asleep in a squalid alleyway in London in the early hours of one freezing November morning. Incredulous, the authors began to investigate the plight of these children and others like them and resolved to make a programme highlighting the horrors they found. The final programme followed the footsteps of two runaways, a girl named Annie and a cheeky 14-year-old named Tommy. Annie had run away at the age of 10 and been raped and became a drug taker and street beggar by the time she was 12. Tommy, a Scots lad, had run away to London, been picked up by a homosexual, posed for pornographic photographs, and ended up in a hostel run by a man named Gleaves. This latter fact was to horrify the millions who watched the programme.

It has been estimated that about 30,000 runaway children arrive in London every year – about 80 every day – and the fate of Annie and Tommy is by no means untypical of what could happen to each and every new arrival. But, although shocked by the plight of these runaway youngsters, TV viewers were stunned by the climax to the two-hour programme.

The TV cameras trailed Tommy to one of several charity hostels run by the seemingly saintly Roger Charles Augustine Gleaves, a 42-year-old ex-grammar-school boy and self-styled Bishop of Medway, a leader of the Old Catholic Church Community Service. (The Old Catholic Church (English Rite) was founded in the 1870s, at a time when many sincere and devout people found themselves unable to accept the newly proclaimed doctrine of Papal Infallibility. It no longer has any connection with the Roman Catholic Church.*)

Roger Gleaves met Tommy at Euston Station and offered the boy a bed in one of the hostels; a large, filthy building that was not even graced with a bath. Gleaves' hostels, some of which were supported by local authorities, were squalid, but at least provided a roof for runaways who would otherwise doss down in a cardboard box in a quiet street.

On the last day of filming the camera crew turned up for work to learn that a boy named Billy McPhee had been horribly beaten in the hostel, then taken away and brutally murdered. His body, with no fewer than twenty stab wounds, had been found in a ditch on the London to Brighton road near Gatwick Airport.

Three hostel wardens were later jailed for life at the Central Criminal Court by Mr Justice MacKenna for the murder of Billy McPhee. Gleaves, who does not seem to have participated in the murder, was later convicted on two counts of assault and two counts of buggery, receiving a sentence of four years. The fate of Billy McPhee is a dramatic example of what can await kids who 'go missing'.

---

*Although established by many sincere Roman Catholics, the Old Catholic Church's introduction to Britain was far from glorious. It was brought to England by a certain Archbishop Mathew, whose fervour for the new movement is said to have had more to do with the fact that he was a defrocked Catholic priest who wanted to get married than with any inability to accept the extension of Papal authority.

It is not too difficult to disappear if you work at it, make meticulous preparations and have luck on your side, but, while disappearing is not impossibly difficult, it cannot be said to be easy. We live in an age where we are all tabbed and documented, and any self-respecting investigator could compile an impressive dossier about a missing person merely by consulting birth records, the files of churches, schools, divorce courts, universities, doctors, dentists, departments of health and social security, hospitals, insurance companies, banks and tax offices, and by talking with employers, neighbours, colleagues, friends and family. And, once armed with this information, the investigator can proceed with his inquiries.

Most people who deliberately disappear change their name, but frequently use their mother's maiden name – or a name that retains their own initials, enabling them to keep articles which bear their monogram.

A detective on the trail of a missing person may begin his search by checking hotels and motels in and near towns with which the missing person is familiar. If these draw a blank he may proceed to make inquiries at accommodation agencies and with the landlords of recently rented flats. Finally, a long shot might be a check with employment agencies and recently advertised vacancies in the missing person's line of work. The investigator's job is made easier by knowledge of the missing person's hobbies, weaknesses and passions, and by those unavoidable twists of fate which suddenly bring a missing person face-to-face with an old friend. To give an example: On 11 April 1976 the *Sunday Express* published a photograph of actor Roger Moore strolling through Berwick Market in Soho, London. Caught in the photograph was a young boy, Robert Williams, a 14-year-old who had been missing from home for seven months. Robert Williams had fallen victim to one of the tricks of fate which can so easily destroy the runaway's best laid plans.

It has been said that you leave a trail behind you wherever you go. Once you have disappeared you must stay in the shadows, never do anything to attract attention, and never achieve anything of interest to others. It is best to abandon your hobbies, find a new career, and generally act as unlike yourself as possible. But even if you go to the most extreme lengths to disappear the chances are that you will be found –

for, as Tracers Inc. of America, a large detective agency specialising in tracing missing persons, contend, no one can successfully disappear if someone loves or hates them enough to pursue the search endlessly.

An example of brilliant detective work occurred in the late 1800s and concerns a Pinkerton Detective named Geyer and the multi-murderer H. H. Holmes. In 1894, Holmes, whose real name was Herman Webster Mudgett, was jailed in Saint Louis for fraud. There he met a vicious train robber named Marion Hedgepath, known as 'the handsomest outlaw in the West', a fast draw who is reputed to have once killed a man whose gun was already drawn before Hedgepath had gone for his own.

Holmes and Hedgepath concocted a scheme to defraud an insurance company: one of Holmes' cohorts, a small-time thief named Benjamin Fuller Pitezel, would rent a house in Philadelphia and erect a sign advertising himself as B. F. Perry, a dealer in patents. He would then take out a life insurance policy with the Mutual Life Insurance Company. Sometime later Holmes would 'acquire' a corpse from a nearby morgue, substitute it for Pitezel and rig a minor explosion. The authorities would investigate, conclude that death was due to an accident, and the insurance company would pay up.

Upon release from prison Holmes, Hedgepath and Pitezel put the scheme into operation. Everything went according to their expectations, with the exception that Holmes, who had never intended getting a corpse from the morgue, actually murdered Pitezel. The body was found and the police concluded that 'B. F. Perry' had died as a result of an accident. Five days later a crooked lawyer friend of Holmes, a man named Jephta D. Howe, arrived in Philadelphia with Pitezel's eldest daughter, Alice, who identified her father's body, apparently unaware of the deception, and collected the insurance money.

H. H. Holmes double-crossed Hedgepath and Howe and disappeared with Alice Pitezel and the money. Hedgepath was furious and revealed the fraud, admitting to his minor rôle in the hope that his display of honesty would induce the court to reduce his sentence – it didn't: he was sentenced to twelve years in prison.

The insurance company now hired the famous Pinkerton

Detectives to run Holmes to ground. A Detective Geyer traced Holmes to Saint Louis, where the murderer had visited Mrs Pitezel, who told Geyer that Holmes had taken her children, 11-year-old Nellie and 9-year-old Howard, to their father and had mentioned something about Cincinnati.

Detective Geyer went to Cincinnati and began a plodding search from hotel to hotel, asking questions and showing photographs of Holmes and the children. He finally found a hotel where a man who fitted Holmes' description had stayed with three children. The man had expressed the intention of going to Toronto, Canada, so Geyer proceeded to that city and began his plodding search afresh, eventually meeting an old gentleman who claimed that a man fitting Holmes' description had rented the house next to his own; H. H. Holmes had only two children with him, however, both of them girls. The old man spoke freely of Holmes, saying that they had got on together quite well. Why, said the man, he'd even loaned Holmes his shovel: Geyer found the bodies of Alice and Nellie Pitezel buried in the cellar of the rented house.

What, though, of the boy, Howard? There was no evidence that he had ever reached Toronto, so Geyer retraced his steps until he arrived in Indianapolis. Here he followed the usual process of checking hotels, but the trail had gone cold. Every hotel in Indianapolis drew a blank and Geyer widened his search to cover neighbouring suburbs; but without success, until only Irvington was left. Here Holmes and three children had rented a house. Neighbours told Geyer several stories about the single father, one of them concerning a new stove installed only a short time before Holmes had left town. Geyer checked: all that remained of Howard Pitezel were a few charred teeth. The boy had ended his days in the stove.

H. H. Holmes was eventually tracked to Boston and arrested. He was later executed at Moyamensing Prison on 7 May 1895. Before he died he admitted to the murder of twenty-seven people. Detective Geyer's remarkable piece of detection is a classic example of just how difficult it is to disappear if there is somebody who loves or hates you enough to pursue an endless search.

Vanishing is by no means easy, yet according to some estimates as many as 100 people vanish in Britain every day! What happens to these people? Are they amnesiacs? Murder victims? Mentally disabled?

The Salvation Army Missing Person Bureau, which solves six out of every ten of its cases, know of only one case of a missing person suffering from amnesia and one case of a missing person being found in a mental institution. And it would seem that murder accounts for only a small percentage of missing people.

The majority of missing people, therefore, deliberately disappear.

1975 was designated International Women's Year, but to those involved in tracing missing people it was known as 'The Year of Vanishing Wives': for the first time more American wives than husbands disappeared. Edward Goldfader, President of Tracers Inc. of America, reported that fifteen years ago male runaways outnumbered females by a ratio of 300 to 1, but that in 1975 the situation dramatically reversed, with twice as many female runaways as male. The cause is thought to have been the Women's Liberation movement, which urged wives to reassess their lives; as a result many wives became disillusioned with the marital scene. These women, many of whom had been married for ten years or more, disappeared to attract attention; a large number left clues to help their husbands find them, some being so blatant as to write a letter to their husbands on notepaper headed with the name of the hotel where they were staying.

According to the Metropolitan Police, a marital breakdown is one of the most common causes of an adult disappearance. Men also vanish to avoid social responsibilities such as supporting a family.

People choose disappearing in preference to some real or imagined threat to their freedom, but there are some reports of people who have disappeared without apparent motive. They are not disgruntled or disillusioned; they are normal, happy folk who are content with life. Yet they disappeared on the spur of the moment, without making any preparations. To make a distinction, these people seem to have done more than just disappear: they have vanished.

2 They Never Came Back

'Vanishing people' are ordinary people, people absorbed with the daily process of living. They are by no means special or of a particular class and their only distinction is that one day they went out – and never came back! Take a look at the following letter, published in *The Times* of 5 August 1873. I don't know whether the ladies mentioned were ever found – one can only hope so – but their disappearance is a perfect example of the 'vanishing person'.

MYSTERIOUS DISAPPEARANCE
To the Editor of The Times

Sir, – In the interest of a family who are suffering the greatest anxiety in consequence of the following most mysterious occurrence, we venture to ask you to assist us by publishing this communication.

On the morning of the 25th June last Mrs Marie Constable, of 26 Seven Sisters Road, Holloway, a lady of independent means, started from home in company with her sister, Mrs Everett, of 13 Grove Road, Holloway, intimating to her servant that they proposed to visit the Alexandra Palace, and would return home for tea. Since that time neither lady has been heard of, nor has any clue been obtained of them, although we have communicated with the police, issued placards and newspaper advertisements offering a reward, caused a thorough search of the grounds and neighbourhood of Alexandra Palace to be instituted, and employed the services of detectives.

All ordinary means having failed, we trust you will, by giving greater publicity to this painful event, increase the probability of intelligence being obtained which may lead to the restoration of the ladies to their friends or their fate being ascertained. The published description is as follows.

Mrs Constable's age is about 55 years, she is about 5 foot 2 inches high, stout, with a ruddy complexion, dark auburn hair, blue eyes, and wore a black silk dress with yellow spots and magenta flowers, trimmed with white satin; gold watch, chain and rings. Mrs Everett's age is about 45; she is 5 feet 3 or 4 inches high, rather masculine, and wore a stone silk dress, black lace shawl, brown hat and feather, side spring boots, and a peculiar gold watch and chain.

We are, sir, your obedient servants, Stoneham and Legge, 5, Philpot Lane, Fenchurch Street, London E.C.

One of the most bizarre writers of recent times was an eccentric American named Charles Fort (1872–1932). His followers have called him 'one sane man in a mad, mad world' and honoured him by establishing the Fortean Society, which still flourishes. He made a hobby of collecting reports of unusual, coincidental, unlikely and supernatural happenings. For twenty-six years he haunted library reading rooms, making notes on all manner of the weird and wonderful, and when he died he left the world a legacy: a new word – 'Fortean', meaning things unexplained and/or ignored by science – and four provocative books, *Book of the Damned, New Lands, Lo!,* and *Wild Talents.*

Lo! is a fund of startling, but documented facts, including some cases of vanishing people. Here is a sample:

Fort records that, on 25 April 1885, the *New York Sun* reported that a young farmer, Isaac Martin, went into one of his fields in Salem, Virginia, and vanished.

In July and August 1892 so many people mysteriously disappeared from Montreal, Canada, that the newspaper headline 'Another Man Is Missing' was common.

In August and September 1893 the *Irish News* reported that five children had disappeared in Belfast. So far as is known, none of the children was ever found and no explanation was offered.

On 5 January 1900, the *Chicago Tribune* reported a search at the Augusta Mills, Battle Creek, Michigan, for a young man named Sherman Church. He had been seen to enter the mill, but nobody had set eyes on him since. The paper says that searchers scoured the surrounding countryside and almost demolished the mill, but failed to find a single clue to either the man's whereabouts or his fate.

Five men mysteriously disappeared from Buffalo in one week, or so the *New York Sun* reported on 14 August 1902.

On the chilly afternoon of 12 December 1910, 25-year-old Dorothy Harriet Camille Arnold, a society-girl member of New York's Four Hundred and niece of United States Supreme Court Justice Rufus L. Peckham, walked off the face of the Earth. At 11.00 am she left her family home at 108 East Seventy-ninth Street on the fashionable East Side of Manhattan to spend the day shopping for an evening dress required for her younger sister's coming-out party some five days hence. Fashionably and expensively dressed, an eye-catching figure, she shopped happily until near two o'clock, when, on Fifth Avenue, one of the busiest streets in the world, she met and chatted for a while with a friend, Gladys King. Their conversation over, Miss King waved goodbye. That was the last time that anybody set eyes on Dorothy Arnold. Many theories have been advanced for the disappearance, ranging from suicide to death at the hands of an illegal abortionist (it being suggested that a boyfriend may have made her pregnant), but her fate has remained a mystery: 'a disappearance which had from the beginning no standard in rationality, being logically both impenetrable and irreconcilable. It remains obstinate and perplexing, a gall to human curiosity, an impossible problem for reason and analytical powers'. Of this disappearance, Charles Fort remarks that on 13 December, the day after Dorothy vanished, the *New York Sun* recorded that a swan appeared on a lake near the 79th Street entrance to Central Park. There was no reference of such an event before and scientists were baffled.

The London *Daily Mirror* recorded that eight children vanished from Belfast in 1920.

Eight people vanished from Southend within days of each other in 1926, reported the *Evening Star* on 2 November. First to go were Mrs Kathleen Munn and her two children. They were quickly followed by four children aged from 15 to 17 years. Finally, a girl named Alice Stevens vanished. She was eventually found in a state of collapse and taken to hospital. The cause of her condition is unknown.

And mysterious disappearances continue.

In 1969 Norfolk police were presented with two classic cases of disappearance. On 8 April, a 14-year-old schoolgirl named April Fabb cycled from her home in Metton to deliver a birthday present to her sister. Her bicycle was found in a field about an hour later, but April was never seen again.

Five months later, in September, 11-year-old Steven Paul Newing also vanished without trace. Neighbours had seen Steven playing with friends in the street near his home in Fakenham during the mid-afternoon. Some twenty minutes later when Steven's mother, Mrs Jean Newing, arrived home from work, the boy had disappeared. The police circulated Steven's description to doctors, dentists and teachers, emphasising a birthmark, an arm that would sometimes dislocate, two front teeth that had been reset after an accident during a football match and occasionally needed treatment, and a scar over his right eye. There were some reports that he had been seen with a bearded man, but these came to nothing. Neither did an appeal to gypsies who had visited a recent sheep fair in the area or a search with tracker dogs of a nearby lime quarry. Steven Paul Newing had vanished without trace.

One Sunday evening in 1974, 26-year-old Carolyn Wright, known to her friends as Patsy, caught the seven o'clock train from London to Liverpool. Tall, slim, attractive and fashionably dressed, she was in the best of spirits; a talented artist with three diplomas, she was about to begin her first term at Liverpool Art College, where she would begin training as a teacher. But she did not reach Liverpool. The police investigated and failed to trace her. 'We are utterly baffled,' admitted a senior police officer. 'When someone disappears there is normally an inkling as to what may have happened. But in this case, nothing.' Two years later, in 1976, there was still no trace of Carolyn Wright.

In February 1975, Jackson Wright and his 36-year-old wife Martha were driving to New York. It had been snowing heavily and a quantity of snow had built up on the windscreen and rear window. On entering the Lincoln Tunnel, Jackson brought the car to a halt. Martha took a cloth and began clearing the rear window, while Jackson wiped the snow off the windscreen. When Jackson looked up from his work his wife was nowhere to be seen. Martha Wright had vanished.

On 5 June 1975, 40-year-old Donald Dent, a stallion keeper at the Red House Stud near Exning, Newmarket, stayed at home because of a sore throat. That evening his wife, 36-year-old Valerie, returned from the village shop where she worked as manageress and found Donald in the living-room watching television. She cooked him a country supper of bacon, eggs, mushrooms and beans, then went upstairs to sit with their 14-year-old son David, who was also unwell.

After spending about forty-five minutes with David, Valerie Dent returned downstairs to make a drink. Donald was still seated in front of the television. Valerie told him that she was very tired and was going to bed. Donald said that he would be up at the end of the programme he was watching. But he did not come up to bed. At 11.30 Valerie returned to the living-room expecting to find her husband asleep in an armchair; she found the television switched on and the front door open. Donald had disappeared.

Mrs Dent spent several hours driving around the lonely lanes of the area in a desperate attempt to find him, but without luck. By dawn the police, joined by gamekeepers and employees of the Red House Stud, mounted an exhaustive search which lasted several days but had to be abandoned without trace of Dent being found.

When Dent vanished he was wearing nothing but a fawn shirt, brown trousers and a pair of heavy working boots. He had no money except what loose change he may have had in his trouser pockets, and he did not take a car. His wife's handbag, containing £30 and the keys to her Ford Cortina, was in the living-room, but Dent didn't touch it.

'The whole thing is a terrible nightmare,' Mrs Dent is reported to have said. 'One minute he was there watching the news and the next minute he had vanished for no reason at all.'

In 1847 the explorer Ludwig Leichardt and his party (equipped with fifty bullocks, twenty mules and seven horses) set out into the central desert of the Australian Outback. Every item, person and animal vanished and, despite repeated searches, not a single trace of the expedition was ever found. The disappearance of Ludwig Leichardt became one of Australia's greatest mysteries – until January 1975. A 40-year-old wild life ranger named Zac Mathias drove into Darwin with photographs of some strange Aboriginal cave paintings of a pipe-smoking white man riding a pony, another white man walking alongside and carrying a saddle, and a third white man being carried by a group of Aborigines. 'We thought the paintings would give us the first positive clue to the disappearonce, 128 years ago, of explorer Ludwig Leichardt and his party,' said Peter Spillet, President of the Northern Territory Historical Society. 'We immediately planned an expedition to the caves and Zac was going to lead us . . . he is the only man who can take us there.'

But Mathias himself disappeared. 'He vanished into thin air and we cannot find him,' said Spillet.

3 The 'Mad Murderer of the Long Trail'

Around Bennington, Vermont, no fewer than seven people disappeared between the years 1945 and 1950. There was no evidence to suggest murder (only one of those to have vanished was ever found – dead, but in a place where it is almost certain that her body would have been found by earlier searchers) but the citizens of Bennington could explain the mysterious events only by inventing a particularly cunning madman, a killer who emerged from nowhere, killed and returned to obscurity until his perverse passions once again drove him to prowl for a fresh victim. To some people this mysterious killer was known as the 'Bennington Ripper', but other people called him (or her) the 'Mad Murderer of the Long Trail'.

This killer derived his name from a hikers' footpath running 262 miles along or not far from the crest of Vermont's Green Mountains. One of the lesser peaks of the mountain chain is Mount Glastonbury, and it was somewhere on the eight miles of trail that goes over the peak that seven people mysteriously vanished.

First to go was a 75-year-old woodsman named Middie Rivers. He is said to have known the Long Trail better than most people know their own living-room, yet on 12 November 1945 he set out to hunt deer and was never seen again. The last that anybody ever saw of him was about twenty miles from the town of Bennington, near the Mount Glastonbury entrance to the trail. Hundreds of people joined the state police in the search: hunters, townsfolk, boy scouts and ninety soldiers from nearby Fort Devens spent a month scouring the region, but the search ended without a trace – without even the slightest clue – of Middie Rivers' fate.

The winter of 1945 came and went. The citizens of

Bennington, involved in the year that passed, forgot about Middie Rivers and ceased to ponder his fate. On 1 December 1946, however, they were forcibly reminded of the bizarre and tragic disappearance when 18-year-old Paula Welden, a student at Bennington College, vanished without trace. Again there was a search and again no clues to her fate were forthcoming.

The 'Mad Murderer' struck again on 1 December 1949, the third anniversary of Paula's disappearance. This time the victim was a man named James E. Telford. There was an extended but once again fruitless search; Telford had vanished like the others – without trace.

Early in 1950 an 8-year-old boy named Paul Jepson was left in his father's truck while Mr Jepson conducted some small errand. He was gone for only a few minutes, but it was long enough for the 'Mad Murderer' to strike. When Jepson returned to his truck his son had vanished. Once again there was a search, and this time bloodhounds were employed, but there occurred a very mysterious thing: the bloodhounds lost Paul Jepson's scent at the exact spot where Paula Welden had last been seen.

Two weeks later an experienced woodswoman named Frieda Langer set out on a hike along the Long Trail with her cousin. She disappeared. Again the police and state police were joined by volunteer searchers and a month was spent searching the snow-covered woods, but without trace of Frieda being found. However, several months later, on 12 May 1951, Frieda Langer's body was found, but it was found in an open and easily visible part of the forest; it couldn't have been overlooked by searchers, yet searchers had overlooked it – or the 'Mad Murderer' had brought the corpse back to the Green Mountains!

On 6 November 1950 a girl named Martha Jeannette Jones disappeared from home. The police were not told for some time because the girl's parents believed that she had run off with a soldier stationed in Virginia. When it was learned that he was as concerned by Martha's absence as were her parents, the police were notified and a search was launched on 12 December.

By this time, however, the 'Mad Murderer' had claimed his seventh victim, a girl named Frances Christman. She had set out to walk three miles to a friend's house, but she never arrived. She was last seen on 3 December and nobody has seen her since.

Of the seven people who vanished, it is the case of Paula Welden which seems to have attracted the most attention, being widely reported in the press at the time and still presenting a baffling mystery. Numerous theories have been advanced: she ran away to escape real or imagined troubles at home; she ran off with a boyfriend; or she was the victim of the 'Mad Murderer'. All are possible, none are proved. Her disappearance presents a challenging mystery.

Bennington College lies in a tranquil 400-acre campus about four miles from the town of Bennington. In 1946 it boasted a student body of roughly three hundred girls aged between seventeen and twenty-two. 18-year-old Paula, a soft spoken and polite girl, the eldest of three daughters of Archibald Welden of Stamford, Connecticut, an industrial engineer employed by the Revere Copper and Brass Company, was not a particularly brilliant student. Her favourite subject appears to have been botany and she often indulged her interest with long, solitary walks. Police later described her as a blue-eyed blonde, about 5ft 5in tall and weighing 123 pounds.

Paula seems to have nurtured a belief that her father cared more for her younger sisters than for herself and resented paying for her expensive education at Bennington College. So far as is known, Paula was not justified in thinking as she did. She seems to have been a sensitive girl and may well have felt dissatisfied with herself as a person. She was no doubt bitten by the same bug that attacks most teenagers: she was 18 years old, neither a child nor yet an adult, and she probably thought a lot about herself on those long walks, her brooding, searching introspection breeding a deeper depression that eventually turned her against her one place of certain security – her home. Indeed, at Thanksgiving she refused to return home and spend the four-day holiday with her family. Maybe that decision made her feel like a martyr, or maybe it was some kind of masochistic penance. Perhaps it has an even deeper significance?

Paula's problems, whatever they may have been, seem to have been forgotten on Saturday, 30 November 1946, the day before she disappeared. That night she attended a house party in the students' quarters and appeared in good spirits – she even grabbed the spotlight with an exhibition of Indian wrestling. Had she therefore come to terms with her problems; was she a manic depressive; or had she seen a solution, in running away, to all her cares?

At midday the next day, Sunday, 1 December, she turned up for work at the Commons, the Bennington College dining hall, where, like several other students, she waited on tables to earn money to help finance her college tuition. At 2.30 she had her own lunch, then returned to her dormitory, where her room-mate, Elizabeth Johnson, was studying. Paula did not get out her own books and join her friend, but instead changed into blue jeans and a red parka with a fur-trimmed hood, and announced that she was going for a walk.

It was a particularly gloomy day. The biting rain of the last few days had turned to sleet and the sky was grey, threatening a snowstorm.

Very little is known about Paula's movements after she left Elizabeth Johnson. She did not return to the college for her evening waitress duties and still hadn't put in an appearance by her usual bedtime. This was most unusual and Elizabeth Johnson grew concerned, but she didn't want to get her room-mate into trouble with the college authorities and so said nothing. By dawn the next day there was still no sign of Paula, and Elizabeth decided to see the Dean.

The Dean suggested that maybe Paula had applied late the previous evening to stay away overnight; it was an unlikely suggestion and a check of the records proved that Paula had not made any such application. The Dean and Elizabeth Johnson then went to the home of Lewis Webster Jones, the President of Bennington College. He made a cautious telephone call to Paula's parents, thinking that Paula might have gone home for some reason, but Paula was not at home and her parents couldn't suggest where their daughter might be. Lewis Webster Jones 'phoned the police.

First to arrive at the college was Clyde W. Peck, the local sheriff. A short time later he was joined by Almo B. Fronzini, a twenty-five year veteran of the Vermont State Police. They searched Paula's room and Elizabeth Johnson confirmed that all Paula's clothes were there except for those she had been wearing when she left. $8.26 was found on Paula's bureau and an uncashed cheque for ten dollars was found in a drawer. Paula rarely possessed more money than this, so it must be assumed that Paula vanished with at most very little money and without taking any extra clothing.

Detective Fronzini took charge of the investigation and rushed off to check the local rail and 'bus stations, thinking that Paula might have had enough cash to buy a ticket. The only interesting shred of information came from the ticket-seller at the rail station. On Sunday afternoon he had sold three hunters tickets to New York City. They had subsequently changed their minds and demanded tickets to Stamford instead. The alteration had caused the ticket-seller to waste considerable time adjusting his records and he therefore clearly remembered the incident. However, apart from the fact that Stamford was Paula's home town, Detective Fronzini could see no collection between Paula and the hunters other than the coincidence of Stamford.

Fronzini returned to Bennington College and joined Sheriff Peck in questioning the students. Had Paula talked about meeting anybody that afternoon? Did she have a boyfriend? Did she have any friends in Bennington with whom she might have gone to stay overnight? Did anybody know of any reason why Paula might have run away? The answer to all their questions was always the same, no.

Paula Welden had not been a particularly inconspicuous figure that wintery afternoon – a lone girl inadequately dressed for the weather, her blonde hair, red coat, blue trousers and white sneakers adding a colourful relief to the drab, rain-misty scenery – but few people had left their firesides that day and only three people came forward to aid the police.

An attendant at the garage opposite the gates of Bennington College recalled having seen a girl dressed in red and blue leave the college gates and run up the path leading to a nearby gravel pit. A few minutes later the girl had reappeared, run back down the path and walked on down Highway 67A, which ran outside the college gates.

At about 3.15 that afternoon a contractor named Louis Knapp, driving hame along Highway 67A, saw a girl fitting Paula's description hitch-hiking, and offered her a lift as far as his home, about three miles from the Mount Glastonbury entrance to the Long Trail. Knapp and the girl chatted, but she restricted her conversation to questions about the Long Trail. According to Knapp, she did not volunteer any information about herself and when Knapp reached his home she thanked him for the lift and walked away.

Paula Welden – for it is unlikely that two girls fitting the same description were wandering around that afternoon – left Louis Knapp at about four o'clock. She was next seen about thirty minutes later when she stopped to ask directions to the Long Trail from Ernest Whitman, the 73-year-old night watchman at the *Banner*, Bennington's local newspaper.

From about 4.30 onwards Paula's movements are unknown. Nobody saw Paula after Ernest Whitman. Nobody that is except, perhaps, the 'Mad Murderer'.

By Wednesday, 4 December, an ever-growing band of volunteers had joined the police searching the Long Trail but the weather was hampering the search. It was cold and beginning to snow heavily, and it promised to get worse. By now few people entertained hopes that Paula would be found alive.

It was at this point in the investigation that a new and distinguished character made his entry into the mystery: District Attorney William Travers Jerome Jnr., a blood relative of Winston Churchill, whose mother had been Jennie Jerome; Jerome's father had been one of the greatest prosecutors in the legal history of New York City.

Another arrival in Bennington that day was Archibald Welden, Paula's father, who had travelled up from Stamford to be near the heart of the search. That night he gave an interview to several newspaper reporters. 'We have not heard from her and have no idea where she could have gone,' he said. 'She was in a mental snarl at the time.' He did not elaborate, nor was he asked to elaborate what he meant by a mental snarl, but it is probable that he was referring to the problems I have already discussed. Asked the inevitable question about boyfriends, he replied: 'It is true that Paula knew many boys, but they were only chums and accompanied her to socials and dances. I know none was serious with her.'

On Thursday, 5 December, seven marine aircraft from the Naval Air Station at Squantum, Massachusetts, planned to fly over the search area, but low-hanging clouds soon forced them to return to base.

Meanwhile, Detective Fronzini had been questioning the handful of people who lived along the Long Trail during the winter months. The Trail was lined with holiday cottages and cabins, but these were left empty during the winter when their owners moved to warmer climes. Only four families braved the bleak, blizzard-prone Trail during the winter and Fronzini received information from two of them.

The first scrap of information was far from exciting; on Sunday night a truck with New York registration plates thundered down the Trail. This was not a particularly rare occurrence and the vehicle had not attracted much attention, but Paula Welden could have been on the Trail at the time and may have accepted a lift.

The second lead was more hopeful. A woman walking along the Trail late Sunday night had been forced to step aside to let a maroon coupé pass by. She had seen a blonde-haired girl in the passenger seat, but had not peered too closely into the passing car because the Long Trail had a reputation as a 'lovers' lane' and middle-aged folk considered it prudent not to stare too closely at the occupants of cars on the Trail at night.

Was Paula the blonde in the maroon coupé? She had already accepted one lift that day and could have accepted another.

That night William Travers Jerome told newsmen that he had ordered a description of the truck with New York registration plates to be broadcast on the radio and published in the press.

On Friday, 6 December, thirty-five employees of the Revere Copper and Brass Company arrived in Bennington to help their colleague to search for his daughter. They joined students from Bennington College, boys from nearby Williams College, Boy Scouts, woodsmen, hunters, townsfolk and the police in a massive search of the eight miles of the Long Trail which stretches over Mount Glastonbury.

A reward for information leading to Paula's discovery had been offered. Contributions from the people of Bennington and elsewhere swelled it to such an extent that it became necessary to start a fund. Over the next seven days the fund reached almost $5,000.

Newspaper coverage of the search for Paula Welden

increased as the days passed, especially in New York where she was dubbed the 'Blonde Soph', and pressmen began to uncover all sorts of clues, most of them of doubtful reliability. It was said that two girls had narrowly escaped the clutches of an amorous male on the Long Trail in 1944; it was rumoured that a Bennington man with a dubious reputation did not have an acceptable alibi; and, of course, the disappearance of woodman Middie Rivers was discussed again.

The weather grew progressively worse and eventually not even the prospect of the reward could tempt cold and weary searchers to brave the misery of the bleak, grey, snow-covered Long Trail. The students of Bennington and Williams Colleges were still enthusiastic, but officials were forced to return them to the classrooms, so only a diminishing band of adults remained to comb the Long Trail. Hope was revived for a while when a pair of panties was found. It was hoped that they might be Paula's, the first clue to the girl's fate, but the police, by methods that we can only wonder at, established that they did not belong to the missing student and people could only speculate about who it was who had lost them on the wintery Long Trail.

During the search, which lasted for over a week, the Bennington police and the State Police followed up every lead and drew a blank each time. Detective Fronzini, William Travers Jerome and Lewis Webster Jones all reluctantly expressed the belief that Paula Welden was dead. Archibald Welden believed – perhaps clung to the hope – that Paula had been kidnapped, but the absence of a ransom note made this a remote possibility. The police admitted defeat and the search ground inexorably to a halt.

A public outcry followed this admission of failure and it was alleged that the Vermont police was inadequate and antiquated. Help was sought from the FBI, but they had no jurisdiction in the case unless or until there was definite evidence that Paula had been kidnapped or murdered, and they were forced to refuse. Governor Dewey of neighbouring New York State was also approached, but he too refused assistance.

Governor Baldwin of Connecticut, Paula's home state, was responsive to the appeals, however, and sent two expert detectives to Bennington. Robert N. Rundle and Dora C.

Scoville began their investigation by asking all the witnesses to retell their story. Nothing new was forthcoming. In fact, nothing new resulted from their investigation.

On Sunday, 15 December, Archibald Welden returned to Stamford with his daughter's belongings. He told newspaper men that he would not return to Bennington 'unless something important comes up'. That night William Travers Jones admitted that the search had ground to a halt. 'All clues have been run down and found unavailing,' he said.

Detective Rundle, who had interviewed the attendant at the petrol station opposite the gate of Bennington College was satisfied that the attendant had seen Paula Welden run up the path to the gravel pit. Rundle also learned that several people had heard a landslide at the pit at about the same time that Paula was seen heading up the path. Rundle therefore suggested that Paula may have precipitated the slide by attempting to scale the 75-foot bank of the pit. He was obviously grabbing at straws since his theory did not account for the fact that the attendant had seen Paula return down the path from the pit and that Knapp and Whitman had both met the girl long after the landslide. However, Rundle's theory gave the police something constructive to do and that night District Attorney Jerome announced that the gravel pit would be excavated the following day.

On Tuesday, 17 December, a large mechanical digger slowly headed up the path towards the gravel pit and began its labourious task of sifting. Paula Welden's body was not found and nothing of interest to the investigators was revealed.

On 23 December, Stamford radio broadcast a poignant plea from Archibald Welden to his daughter: 'Paula, in just two more days it will be Christmas. If this appeal reaches you, know that we love you. Whatever prompted you to leave us, if you have gone of your own free will, be sure that we can find a better answer to your problems by working on it together. Wherever you are just pick up the nearest 'phone and ask for me. You won't need money. Just ask the operator to reverse the charges. I will come for you immediately, wherever you are, and bring you home to your mother and sisters who love you and miss you so terribly.' Mr Welden's plea was greeted by silence.

Christmas passed and a miserable one it must have been for

the Welden family. In May, Archibald Welden returned to Bennington and again organised a search of the Long Trail. For two days searchers plodded through incessant rain and splashed through muddy puddles left by the thawed winter snows in the hope of finding some clue overlooked during the bad weather. Nothing was found. A despondent Mr Welden left Bennington and did not return. He said that he was satisfied that everything that could be done had been done.

The last possible clue to Paula's fate came in the Spring when a maroon coupé was found abandoned in upper New York State. A check with the State Motor Vehicle Bureau revealed that the car had been stolen from Troy, New York, late the previous year. Could that maroon coupé have been the one with a blonde-haired passenger seen on the Long Trail on the day Paula disappeared? Nobody knows. The car bore no clues.

What happened to Paula Welden? The mystery deepens when we try to attach some logic to Paula's behaviour that afternoon. She left the college inadequately dressed for the weather, suggesting that she did not intend to be away for long, and headed up the path towards the gravel pit, indicating that the Long Trail was not her original destination. A keen botanist, Paula was surely familiar with the countryside around Bennington and it seems inconceivable that she was unfamiliar with the Long Trail, one of Vermont's principal attractions, yet she questioned both Knapp and Whitman about the Trail, asking questions to which she surely knew the answers. What explanation is there to this behaviour? She may simply have changed her mind about going to the gravel pit and could merely have been making polite conversation with Knapp, but, setting aside the possibility that she was genuinely unfamiliar with the Long Trail, she had no possible reason for questioning Ernest Whitman.

I cannot help but wonder if Paula had a secret assignation that afternoon. Let us suppose that Paula, feeling starved of affection and seeking approval, met a man, one of Bennington's 11,257 residents or one of the summer visitors who vacation on the Long Trail. This man was probably older than Paula (maybe even married), which would explain why his presence was kept a secret – neither Paula's father nor the college authorities would approve of her association with an older man. At Thanksgiving, when Paula refused to spend the holiday with her parents, Paula's behaviour may not have been out of spite, as her parents thought, but so that she could meet her new friend. Perhaps they talked about running away and starting a new life together. They may well have arranged to meet that Sunday afternoon near the gravel pit, which would explain Paula's high spirits at the house party the previous evening.

Let us suppose that this man grew tired of Paula's attentions or afraid that their relationship would be discovered by his wife. He tried to end their friendship but Paula became upset and maybe made some kind of threat. He backpedalled, saying that he would arrange for them to run away together. That Sunday afternoon he met Paula at the gravel pit and told her to head for the Long Trail and drew attention to herself by asking directions from everyone she met, deliberately laying a false trail. At the entrance to the Trail they met and drove off together, perhaps in a maroon coupé. But, instead of driving her off to a love nest, Paula's man took her to a hole in the ground.

This is one theory of many. It takes into account the peculiarities of her behaviour that afternoon, but it also assumes a great deal. It may be simpler to assume that Paula, depressed again, went for a walk, heading for the gravel pit, and decided to run away. Maybe she planned to walk the Long Trail, staying overnight in the hikers' huts which line the Trail no more than a day's hike apart. She might even have planned this move, hiding some food and extra clothing at the gravel pit. Maybe she succeeded and is now living, or maybe she fell and injured herself in some remote spot, dying from starvation or exposure.

Other theories suggest that she was killed by a hit-and-run driver who hid her body; that she was kidnapped and killed when her abductors grew alarmed by the publicity; or that maybe a homicidal maniac did roam the Long Trail.

Paula Welden was the second of seven people who vanished on the Long Trail. Each disappearance was followed by an exhaustive search, but, with one exception, none of the bodies were found. The 'Mad Murderer', if such a fiend existed,

suddenly stopped his crimes in 1950. It is said that some
killers, Jack the Ripper types, eventually kill themselves.
Perhaps suicide was the fate of the 'Mad Murderer'. On the
other hand, maybe the cold of wintery Vermont drove the
'Mad Murderer' to somewhere warmer.

In 1956 a series of inexplicable disappearances took place
in the rugged 690,000 acre wilderness of California's Angels
National Forest, specifically from a region known as the
Devil's Gate Reservoir. The victims were children, which gave
the area the sinister name of the 'Forest of Disappearing
Children'.

The disappearances began on 5 August 1956, when two
youngsters, Donald Lee Baker and Brenda Howell, vanished
without trace. A little over seven months later, on 23 March
1957, 8-year-old Tommy Bowman, walking down a forest
trail just ahead of his father, sister, uncle and two cousins,
walked around a bend. He was only a few paces ahead of his
family, but it was a few paces too many. Tommy Bowman
vanished. Over four hundred volunteer searchers descended
on the area and every foot of the trail was examined. Low-
flying helicopters crossed and recrossed the area time and
again. The region of Devil's Gate rang with the cries of
searchers, but there was no answering cry. Tommy had been
only a few paces ahead of his family. If he had fallen or been
snatched they should have heard a cry or the sound of a
scuffle, but they heard nothing and Tommy Bowman vanished
as if he'd stepped through a doorway to another world.

On 13 July 1960, Bruce Kremen, just nine days short of
his ninth birthday, went on his first YMCA hike. Despite his
enthusiasm and determination the pace of the older boys was
too much and he was forced to return to camp. The patrol
leader took Bruce to the camp's perimeter and left him to
walk the last few yards into camp alone. A few yards, but the
last yards that Bruce Kremen ever walked. He never reported
to the camp leaders as instructed. He was never seen again.
The subsequent search lasted twelve days, but not a trace of
the boy was ever found.

4 They Vanished in Front of Witnesses

What happened to Paula Welden and the victims of the 'Forest of Disappearing Children'? Were they the prey of a particularly clever and perverse criminal, a kidnapper or a wild animal, or did they meet with an accident? The police investigated every possibility and followed up every line of inquiry, but in these cases – and in thousands like them – had to abandon their inquiries without a clue as to the missing person's fate. Paula Welden and the others vanished – but is it possible that they literally vanished; that is, suddenly and inexplicably ceased to exist? Some people believe that it is possible for people to vanish and they invariably cite one or more of the following cases as proof.

James Burne Worson, the jogging shoemaker
James Burne Worson lived in Leamington Spa, a health resort, noted for its saline springs, about eight miles from Coventry. He was a shoemaker and a health fanatic, although most of his exercise seems to have consisted of boasting about his physical prowess over a pint of beer with his friends. At least that was the case until one day in 1873, when three of his friends, having grown weary of his unsubstantiated claims, called his bluff and wagered that he could not run to Coventry and back. Worson, of course, accepted the challenge and his friends demanded that he set off immediately, a somewhat daunting task for somebody who had been supping ale.

Worson's friends, a linendraper named Barham Wise, a photographer named Hammerson Burns, and a third man whose name is not recorded, clambered into a light cart and followed the jogging shoemaker, making sure that he remained faithful to the terms of the wager. They also planned to enjoy a few hours of innocent sport at Worson's expense, little imagining that the afternoon's entertainment would soon turn into a nightmare.

It was a warm afternoon but Worson jogged along the dusty road without complaint and without showing any signs of fatigue. With a growing respect for his stamina, his friends shouted jeers or words of encouragement as the spirit moved them. The shoemaker jogged on, covering several miles and spurred forward by the cries ringing in his ears.

Worson jogged ahead of the rambling cart, happily maintaining his pace and apparently unconcerned by the heat of the afternoon. His friends, bumping along after Worson, were watching closely for any sign that he was about to give up when Worson suddenly seemed to stumble over some unseen object. He tripped, cried out and – vanished!

The men in the cart did not – could not – believe their eyes. For a few moments they sat in stunned silence before jumping from the cart and running to the spot where their friend had disappeared. There was no hole in the road into which Worson could have fallen, and the road ahead and behind was empty. They called Worson's name, admitted that his trick had fooled them, called off the wager, even agreed to pay the bet if only Worson would reveal himself. But Worson did not appear.

The three men eventually gave up searching and returned to Leamington Spa, where they went straight to the authorities and told their bizarre story. The police investigated and questioned the witnesses very thoroughly on several occasions, but their story could not be shaken. They steadfastly maintained that James Burne Worson had vanished in front of their eyes.

To this day the testimony of Worson's friends stands as the recorded testimony of the shoemaker's fate: he vanished in front of witnesses.

Is this incredible story true? Did Worson vanish in front of the startled eyes of three friends? Or did his friends murder him? It would not be the first time that a murderer had reported his victim missing, but there is a world of difference between reporting somebody missing and reporting that somebody has just vanished in front of your eyes. If Burns, Wise, and the unnamed third man did murder Worson, then theirs must be one of the most bizarre alibis in criminal history.

An alternative solution to this incredible tale is that James Burne Worson never existed and that the whole story is the product of some unknown person's fertile imagination. A record of all births, deaths and marriages since 1837 in England and Wales has been kept at St Catherine's House, London. I consulted the records there for 1871 to 1875, but could not find any mention of James Burne Worson. Perhaps, then, he never existed – or maybe his death was never recorded!

The Mystery of David Lang

Few lovers of mysteries will be unfamiliar with the frequently reported case of David Lang, a farmer who lived in a large, vine-covered farmhouse on the 'Old Cottontown Road' near Gallatin in Sumner County, Tennessee. One day in 1880, when crossing one of his fields, David Lang vanished. Five people witnessed the event, dozens of neighbours joined the search for him, hundreds came to ponder his fate, and millions have since read about his disappearance and speculated.

On 23 September 1880, Lang returned to his farm from a trip to nearby Nashville. He had brought a present for his children, 11-year-old Sarah and 8-year-old George: a little toy wagon pulled by wooden horses. The children were playing with this in the front yard when Lang vanished. Their mother was watching them, enjoying their obvious delight with the new toy. Lang was walking across the forty-acre pasture in front of the house, heading for the far end of the field where he kept a team of superb horses, his pride and joy.

Lang was halfway across the pasture when a buggy turned into the long lane towards the house. It contained two old friends of the family, a Gallatin lawyer named Judge August Peck and his brother-in-law, a man named Wade, from Akron, Ohio. They both saw Lang and waved. Mrs Lang looked to see if David had seen them. He was returning their wave and turning back towards the farmhouse. He took a few steps – and vanished.*

*An article of dubious authenticity, 'How Lost Was My Father', which claims to be based on an account by Lang's daughter of the disappearance, paints a slightly different picture. Mrs Lang was standing on the porch above the children, who were arguing over their new toy, when she suddenly screamed and the children ran up to the porch to see what had happened. Therefore, it would appear that only three people actually saw David vanish.

A Sumner County surveyor who subsequently examined the field at Judge Peck's request declared that there was a solid limestone base without sinkholes or hidden entrances to underground caves and it was obvious to everyone that the pasture was unmarked by trees or bushes. David Lang vanished as if he had walked through a doorway into another world.

Mrs Lang reached the spot where David had vanished and had hysterics. Judge Peck, trying to comfort her, took her back to the farmhouse and summoned a certain Doctor Anthony who treated her for shock. Meanwhile, somebody began ringing a large bell in the yard to alert neighbours to an emergency. By nightfall the pasture was covered with searchers, their lanterns flickering ghost-like in the still night air. They turned every pebble and inspected every blade of grass, but found not a clue to David's fate.

As the weeks passed the Lang farm was visited by hordes of rubber-necked curiosity-seekers, among them the writer Ambrose Bierce (who later himself disappeared). The farm employees, however, could not get away fast enough, being afraid that they might be the next victims of the whatever-it-was that had 'got' David, and it was several months before the farm returned to some semblance of sanity under the management of Judge Peck. Mrs Lang never recovered; she was bedridden for the rest of her life and would never admit that her husband was dead. Although she allowed the farm to be sold, she refused to let anybody touch the forty-acre pasture in front of the house.

But perhaps stranger, more bizarre than the disappearance itself, was the experience of Lang's children, Sarah and George, a year after David vanished. They noticed a ring of stunted yellow grass about fifteen feet in diameter on the spot where their father had vanished. For some reason Sarah called her father's name and, to her astonishment, heart a faint reply, her father's voice calling for help, over and over, until it faded away and was never heard again.

The years rolled by, Mrs Lang remained bedridden, the farm was sold and the children went to live with their grandparents in Virginia. George later joined the army, married and began his own family. Sarah went to finishing school in Baltimore, but unlike George she continued to seek a solution to her father's fate – and eventually found one, although she states in the article 'How Lost Was My Father' that her brother, who had never had much sympathy with her search, did not accept it.

Upon leaving finishing school, Sarah developed an interest in spiritualism, which she hoped might reveal her father's fate. She spent thousands of dollars cultivating the most famous mediums, but there was a noticeable lack of success until, at a small seance in Philadelphia, she received a message from her mother: 'She says that she is seeking what you are seeking,' said the medium, 'and that she is waiting as you are waiting. And she says you can come to her directly . . .'

After much deliberation Sarah realised that the message meant that her mother was also seeking David's fate and that in future she, Sarah, could establish direct contact with the afterlife. Months of practice failed to develop any latent psychic powers, however, and it wasn't until Sarah was given a planchette – an automatic writing device – that she established contact with her mother. The following years failed to elicit any news of David and in 1926 financial worries destroyed Sarah's powers of concentration, preventing her from contacting her mother. Three years passed, then, at 10 o'clock one morning in April 1929, a strange force compelled her to take up the planchette once more. Under her fingers the small pencil dashed furiously, finally steadied and wrote: 'Together now and forever . . . after many years . . . God bless you.'

The writing was not her mother's. Could it be her father's? Sarah fetched a copy of Charles Lamb's *Tales From Shakespeare* from her trunk of childhood souvenirs. There, on the flyleaf, was an inscription: 'To Sarah, on her tenth birthday, from her father.' The handwriting matched that on the planchette. At last David Lang was reunited with his wife.

Much of the information contained in this account – and all the details of Sarah's experiences with the planchette – come from the article 'How Lost Was My Father' by Stuart Palmer which appeared in the July 1953 issue of *Fate* magazine. In a letter dated 28 May 1952, to a Mr Webster (a pseudonym of Curtis Fuller, editor of *Fate*), Palmer says that the article is a rewrite of a story he had written years ago for *Ghost*, a small magazine published between 1936 and 1937. It is supposed to be a first-person account as told to Palmer by Sarah Lang in 1931, when she was aged about 61. 'It is pretty much the way the old girl told it to me,' says Palmer, 'using her own language and her own prim, old-fashioned phrases as much as possible.' He continues: 'I felt a sort of sincerity in her and cannot believe that she would go to all the trouble of concocting a hoax. I myself saw the original documents – the scrawled page on which the planchette is supposed to have written its message, and the little faded book of Lamb with its inscription. Unfortunately they are no longer extant – I returned the book to Miss Lang.' As proof of the story's authenticity, however, there is an affadavit signed by both Palmer and Sarah Lang and witnessed by a notary public.

A Fortean investigator named Robert Schadewald became interested in the Lang case after noticing certain similarities in the handwriting on the affadavit and the planchette and Sarah's childhood book (all of which were reproduced with Palmer's article). He submitted the handwriting samples to Ann B. Hooten of Minneapolis, a nationally known Examiner of Questioned Documents and member of the prestigious American Society of Document Examiners. Mrs Hooten, who is fully qualified in handwriting, typescript, paper and ink analysis, returned a five-page report in which she stated that the results of her examination proved conclusively that the accumulated writings were from the same individual.

With regard to the affadavit, the notary public's name is neither typed nor stamped on it, nor does it bear a notary's seal. Furthermore, a notary public's task is not hampered by any obligation to verify the truth of what he is told. He merely signs to confirm that an individual giving information has taken an oath to the effect that the given information is true.

Further research into the Lang case was undertaken by Hershel G. Payne, a librarian at the Public Library of Nashville and Davidson County, who was naturally interested in this acclaimed local incident. He checked the census records for 1880 (1880 Census of Sumner County, Surveyor's District 3, Enumeration District 219, of the 13th District of Sumner County). Such a census was taken every ten years and was taken in Sumner County approximately three months before the alleged disappearance of David Lang. Neither the name of Lang nor the name of Peck appear in the records. The only similar name that might have been mistaken for Lang is Sang, but there is no mention of a David, Emma, Sarah or George.

Also, there is no mention of a Lang or Peck in the records for either 1830 or 1850.

The census records are very reliable, although not infallible. For example, the Lang family could have been away from home when the census taker called and Judge Peck could have been an itinerant Judge travelling from place to place and domiciled in another county altogether. However, many friends and acquaintances are said to have joined in the search for David Lang and one would thus expect the Lang family to have been well established in the area, so somebody would surely have given details of the Langs to the census taker.

Nevertheless, the census could be in error, so Mr Payne took a drive along the 'Old Cottontown Road' where the Lang farm was supposed to have been located. In his words, 'I had a beautiful drive – nothing more.' Not satisfied, Mr Payne contacted the Sumner County historians and the Librarian of the Gallatin Public Library, who in turn contacted other knowledgeable persons: all stated that there were no descriptions or pictures of the Lang farm, no documents attesting to the existence of either Lang or Judge Peck, and no contemporary accounts of the disappearance.

The evidence for the Lang disappearance therefore depends on Stuart Palmer's article in *Fate*, and the authenticity of that is questionable. Where, then, did the story originate? Mr Payne believes that it was first told by a travelling salesman called Joe Mulhatten. It seems that in the 1880s the folk of Sumner County were entertained by lying contests in which men vied for the title 'Biggest Liar'. Mulhatten was the champion and his story about David Lang his biggest lie. He is said to have sold the tale to the *Cincinnati Enquirer* (all copies for the 1880s are on microfilm, but there is no index, so it could take weeks to locate the item – if it exists: a job open to any researcher who wants a challenge!). From there it may have been picked up by other papers and printed as fact. One of the accounts could have been the source of the idea for Ambrose Bierce's story 'The Difficulty Of Crossing A Field', which appeared in his book *Can Such Things Be?*, published in 1893, and was said to be based on a true incident. Bierce may have given Stuart Palmer the idea for his story in *Ghost* and, later, *Fate*. Palmer is credited as a source by the well known psychic researcher Nandor Fodor, who told a version of the Lang story in the December 1956 issue of *Fate*. From there on the story has been told dozens of times. The English writer Harold T. Wilkins told it in his book *Strange Mysteries Of Time And Space*, claiming that it was summarised from several contemporary newspapers, which he does not name. A year later Frank Edwards used the Lang case to begin his very popular book *Stranger Than Science*, and it is this account which seems to have been the main source of other writers, who used the story assuming that *somebody* had verified it.

A trilogy of water-carriers

16-year-old Charles Ashmore lived in Quincey, Illinois, a town on the Mississippi River about ninety-five miles from the State Capital, Springfield. One night in November 1878 Charles went into the yard of his home to fetch a pail of water from the well. After an undue length of time had passed without his return, his father, Christian, grabbed a lantern and went to the porch. 'Charles!' he called. 'Charles! Charles!' But there was no reply. Christian was joined at the porch by Martha, his eldest daughter, and they both peered into the winter darkness, calling the boy's name. Christian raised the lantern, but its feeble, flickering light barely invaded the enveloping darkness.

A light snow had fallen and the boy's footprints had left a clear trail. Followed by Martha, Christian traced his son's footprints, but they came to an abrupt end halfway to the well. Beyond, sideways and backwards was an unbroken blanket of crisp, white snow.

Little could be done that night, but at first light the Ashmore family began a thorough search of the yard. They looked everywhere and investigated every possibility.

Charles Ashmore was never *seen* again, but he was heard! Four days after he'd vanished his mother heard him calling for help. She began a frantic search of the yard, continually calling her son's name, but the voice kept moving about and Mrs Ashmore finally fled into the house in hysterics. The strange phenomenon continued for several days and the voice was heard by all the Ashmore family, several friends and a number of neighbours, all of whom agreed that the voice was definitely that of Charles. Eventually the voice grew fainter and eventually faded away completely.

11-year-old Oliver Larch, our second water-carrier, lived in South Bend, Indiana, on the south bend of the St Joseph River, and he is said to have vanished in circumstances similar to Charles Ashmore – so similar, in fact, that many people believe that both stories have the same origin.

Oliver Larch vanished shortly before midnight on Christmas Eve 1889. He had gone into the yard of his home to fetch a pail of water and a few minutes later was heard calling 'Help! Help! They've got me!' Oliver's parents rushed outside and saw their son's footprints in the snow – but they went only halfway to the well. Oliver Larch was never seen again.

The third boy to vanish while fetching a bucket of water was 11-year-old Oliver Thomas, the son of a farmer named Owen Thomas; the scene of the abduction was the yard of the Thomas farmhouse near the small market town of Rhayader in Wales.

It was Christmas Eve (again), 1909. Shortly before midnight Owen sent Oliver into the yard to fetch a bucket of water. The boy had been gone for a few moments when he was heard to cry out, 'Help! Help! They've got me!' The search for Oliver Thomas was identical to the searches for Ashmore and Larch: a flickering lantern sending ghostly shadows across the snow-covered ground and revealing a trail of footprints leading halfway to the well and no further.

What was it that had 'got' the boy? Why did he shout 'they' rather than 'it', or 'something', or just plain 'help'? Does Oliver's choice of words indicate that he knew who his abductors were? And whoever 'they' were, why didn't they leave a trail in the snow? These are just some of the many questions that have been asked – and for my part I am not convinced that we need waste time trying to answer them. The disappearances of Ashmore, Larch and Thomas are so similar that they must be duplicate accounts of the same story, although which if any is the original is anybody's guess.

Oliver Thomas was 11 years old when he vanished in 1909, so he would have been born in 1898 and both his birth and death certificates should be on file at St Catherine's House, but a search through the records for 1897 to 1899 and 1908 to 1911 failed to produce any mention of Oliver Thomas of Rhayader, Wales.

5 The Missing Battalion

One of the most amazing accounts of a disappearance was told in 1965 by Frederick Reichardt. He claimed that in 1915, during the fated Gallipoli Campaign, he had seen a British Battalion (he says it was a Regiment, but this is patently an error), later identified as the First-Fourth Norfolk, march into a strange cloud which was straddling a dry creek bed. The men marched into the cloud without hesitation, but not one of them was seen to emerge. After the last man had entered, the cloud lifted, joined several similarly shaped clouds and moved off against the wind. Not one of the First-Fourth Norfolk was ever seen again!

Since 1965 this story has been told many times, particularly in books about UFOs, yet it would appear that none of the tellers did much by way of research. If they had, they would have learned that the First-Fourth Norfolk did not disappear in 1915 or at any time thereafter. However, it is an undisputed historical fact that over 200 members of the First-*Fifth* Norfolk did vanish at Gallipoli, their fate never having been ascertained. Is it therefore possible that Reichardt, no matter how unbelievable his story, did in fact witness the fate of the First-Fifth and mistakenly identify them as the First-Fourth? Or is his story a complete fabrication, and, if so, what was the fate of the missing soldiers?

The Mediterranean and the Black Sea are connected by the Dardanelles, a long, narrow channel extending about forty miles along the Gallipoli Peninsula. In 1915, following an alliance between Turkey and Germany, control of the Dardanelles became a coveted prize. As far as the Allies were concerned, possession would cut the Turkish Empire in half; open a supply route to Russia when her northern ports were closed by ice; sever German communications with the Middle East; secure the defence of Egypt; and enable the Allies to surround the Central Powers with an iron circle.

Gallipoli was possibly the worst battleground in the War. In spring and early summer the Peninsula is exquisitely beautiful. Charming, toy-like villages nestle between hills ablaze with colourful flowers and the whole picturesque scene is set against the deep blue of the Dardanelles. But, as summer progresses, the enchantment dies, the flowers fade, the grass withers and the relentless sun burns the ground a yellow-brown. From the end of April until October Gallipoli is one of the most inhospitable places on Earth. The Norfolk battalions arrived in the height of the hellish summer.

The First-Fourth and First-Fifth Norfolk were Territorials – 'Saturday Night Soldiers' to the men of the Regular Army – but they belonged to a Regiment with a proud history stretching back over 200 years to the time of Monmouth's Rebellion in 1685, when the Norfolk Regiment was raised by James II, who called them Colonel Henry Cornwall's 9th Regiment of Foot. They prepared for war at Dereham, a small market town not far from Norwich, as part of the predominantly East Anglian 163rd Brigade (which was composed of the First-Fourth and First-Fifth Norfolk, First-Eighth Hampshires and First-Fifth Suffolk – all Territorials) of the 54th Division. They embarked for the Dardanelles on 29 July 1915, and got their first sight of the Gallipoli Peninsula on 10 August. It was not a sight that even the most war-hardened soldier would easily forget.

As they approached Suvla Bay, a long, narrow beach running for about a mile along the west coast of the Peninsula, they could see the carcasses of dead horses and mules floating in the sea. The Navy made periodic attempts to sink them by puncturing them with bayonettes or by churning them up in the ship's propellers, but when these attempts failed the hideously mangled carcasses were left; a grim warning of the horrors to be encountered on land.

A short distance from the beach is a large salt lake. Dry in summer, it reflects the sun's rays with a harsh glare that cruelly assails the eyes and from which there is precious little relief. Beyond lay the battlefield: hard ground dissected by dried water courses and broken here and there by a few stunted olive trees. In the distance a triangle of bleak hills stretched from north to south in a semicircle which gave the plain the appearance of a giant arena. To the north was Kiretch Tepe, to the east the twin heights of Kavak Tepe and Tekke Tepe, and to the south was Sari Bair. As the ground began to rise towards these hills there were belts of thick, prickly scrub, and as the ground rose sharply towards the mountain heights progress was confined to narrow, winding goat tracks.

Conditions here were appalling: corpses lay about in great numbers, burial was rudimentary to say the least, and it was not uncommon to feel the squelching softness of a barely buried body underfoot or to see a hand or a face protruding from the ground. The military situation was also bad. The Allies were sick, exhausted and disheartened, poised on the brink of defeat. It is a matter of historical record that they would evacuate the Peninsula before the end of the year, but at the time of the Norfolk's arrival it was believed that fresh troops might turn the tide of the campaign.

While it was not normal practice to plunge 'green' troops into battle without giving them time to grow accustomed to combat in a quiet sector, Sir Ian Hamilton, Commander-in-Chief of the Mediterranean Expeditionary Force, believed that any delay might cost the Allies victory and so went ahead with plans for a major offensive involving the 54th Division (of which the Norfolks were a part) and the 53rd Division, which had arrived during the night of 8/9 August. He envisaged a bold, sweeping assault on the twin heights of Kavak and Tekke Tepe, the central slice of the mountain heights that dominated Suvla Plain. In a dispatch to Lord Kitchener, the Secretary of State for War, he described his proposition and the results:

I proposed that the 54th Division should make a night march in order to attack, at dawn on the 13th, the heights Kavak Tepe and Tekke Tepe. The Corps Commander having reason to believe that the enclosed country about Kuchuk Anafarta Ova and to the north of it was held by the enemy, ordered one brigade to move forward in advance, and make good Kuchuk Anafarta Ova, so as to ensure an unopposed night march for the remainder of the division as far as that place.

In other words, Sir Ian Hamilton proposed that during the night of 12/13 August the 54th Division should march as far as the foothills of Kavak Tepe and Tekke Tepe; then, at dawn on the 13th, boldly attack the twin heights. However, the Corps Commander, Lt-Gen Sir Frederick Stopford, maintained that a cultivated area known as Kuchuk Anafarta Ova was held by enemy snipers and suggested that a single battalion should move forward during the afternoon of 12 August and clear the enemy from the area, ensuring an unopposed night march by the rest of the brigade.

It was accordingly arranged that, at four o'clock in the afternoon on Thursday, 12 August 1915, the 163rd Brigade would advance and, with support from naval guns, an 18-pounder battery and a battery of mountain guns, clear Kuchuk Anafarta Ova of enemy snipers. They would then position themselves about 2,000 yards east of a place on the map known as Point 28, whereupon another brigade would move forward and consolidate the position. The whole division would then advance under cover of darkness and attack the twin heights at dawn.

The advance that afternoon was a fiasco from beginning to end. Worse, it was an incompetent muddle. The commanders believed that Suvla Plain was only lightly held by the enemy, but in fact the area was totally unreconnoitred and the strength and disposition of the enemy completely unknown. Commanding officers had never seen the ground over which the advance was to take place, and most of the maps hurriedly issued at the last moment depicted another part of the Peninsula. And, finally, the advance was delayed by forty-five minutes, but faulty communications prevented the artillery support from being informed. They accordingly opened fire on schedule, thus depriving the advance of whatever support the artillery might have given.

Nevertheless, at 4.45 pm the 163rd Brigade began their advance. On the left flank Lt-Col W. M. Armes led the First-Fifth Suffolk; in the middle were the First-Eighth Hampshires (known as the Isle of Wight Rifles) led by Lt-Col J. E. Rhodes; and on the right flank came the First-Fifth Norfolk. The First-Fourth Norfolk, led by their adjutant, brought up the rear.

The First-Fifth Norfolk were commanded by Sir Horace Beauchamp, an ardent cavalry soldier of the old school who

had seen action in Egypt, the Sudan and South Africa. He was
known as 'the bos'n' because of his passionate love of the sea,
and must be one of the few cavalry officers to have once
devoted his leave to standing watch on an ocean liner to qualify
for a Master Mariner's certificate. He had retired in 1904, but
like so many old soldiers he emerged from retirement to take
command of a fighting company.

The brigade moved forward, but had advanced no more
than about 1,000 yards when the main body ran into heavy
machine-gun fire and was forced to ground. The right flank,
however, found themselves less strongly opposed and charged
ahead, Sir Horace Beauchamp waving his cane in the air and
urging them onward.

Sir Ian Hamilton described the following events in a dispatch
to Kitchener:

> In the course of the fight, creditable in all respects to the
> 163rd Brigade, there happened a very mysterious thing. The
> First-Fifth Norfolk were on the right of the line, and found
> themselves for the moment less strongly opposed than the rest
> of the brigade. Against the yielding forces of the enemy
> Colonel Sir H. Beauchamp, a bold, self-confident officer,
> eagerly pressed forward, followed by the best part of the
> battalion. The fighting grew hotter, and the ground became
> more wooded and broken. At this stage many men were
> wounded or grew exhausted with thirst. These found their
> way back to camp during the night. But the Colonel, with
> 16 officers and 250 men, still kept pushing forward, driving
> the enemy before him. Amongst these ardent souls was part
> of a fine company enlisted from the King's Sandringham
> estates. Nothing more was seen or heard of any of them.
> They charged into the forest and were lost to sight or sound.
> Not one of them ever came back.

The failure of the advance that afternoon crushed Sir Ian
Hamilton's hopes of turning the tide of the campaign, and
the Peninsula had to be evacuated before the end of the year.
205,000 British and 47,000 French were killed, wounded,
missing, dead from disease and evacuated sick. For those who
survived, the war had only just begun and the horrors of the
Western Front lay ahead. A few months later the Government

appointed a Royal Commission to investigate the causes of the defeat. Almost everyone involved in the initiation of the campaign was interviewed, a notable exception being Lord Kitchener, who had been drowned aboard the *Hampshire* in the North Sea. *The Final Report Of The Dardanelles Commission* was made available in 1917, but it was heavily censored. A second edition, still censored, was released in 1919, and it was not until 1965 that a declassified edition was released – a not insignificant date, as we shall see.

At the end of the war the Allies returned to Gallipoli and on 23 September 1919 it seemed that the mystery of the missing Norfolks had been solved when an officer commanding a British Graves Registration Unit triumphantly announced: 'We have found the 5th Norfolk! There were 180 in all. The bodies were scattered over an area of about one square mile at a distance of 800 yards behind Turkish lines.' The bodies were found when a soldier of the Occupation Forces was touring the battlefield and found a badge of the Royal Norfolk Regiment. He made some enquiries and learned that a Turkish farmer had removed 180 bodies from his property – many from within his farmhouse, where the 163rd brigade presumably made their last stand – and deposited them in a nearby ravine.

Most accounts of the events that August afternoon end here, but it is obvious that a mystery still exists. Not all the missing Norfolks were found. In fact, only 122 of the bodies were Norfolks, which leaves 145, more than half the battalion, unaccounted for. Nobody knows what happened to those men. The mystery was forgotten and remained so for nearly fifty years.

In 1965 a veteran of Gallipoli, Mr Frederick Reichardt, told the following story:

August 21, 1915
The following is an account of the strange incident that happened on the above date, which occurred in the morning during the severest and final period of fighting which took place on Hill 60, Suvla Bay, ANZAC.

The day broke clear, without a cloud in sight, as any beautiful Mediterranean day could be expected to be. The exception, however, was a number of perhaps six or eight 'loaf of bread' shaped clouds – all shaped exactly alike – which were hovering over Hill 60. It was noticed that, in spite of a four or five mile an hour breeze from the south, these clouds did not alter their position in any shape or form, nor did they drift away under the influence of the breeze. They were hovering at an elevation of about 60 degrees as seen from our observation point 500 feet up. Also stationary and resting on the ground right underneath this group of clouds was a similar cloud in shape, measuring about 800 feet in length, 220 feet in height, and 200 feet in width. This cloud was absolutely dense, solid looking in structure, and positioned about 14 to 18 chains from the fighting in British-held territory. All this was observed by 22 men of No. 3 Section, No. 1 Field Company, N.Z.E., including myself, from our trenches on Rhododendron Spur, approximately 2,500 yards south west of the cloud on the ground. Our vantage point was overlooking Hill 60 by about 300 feet. As it turned out later, this singular cloud was straddling a dry creek bed or sunken road [Kaiajik Dere] and we had a perfect view of the cloud's sides and ends as it rested on the ground. Its colour was a light grey, as was the colour of the other clouds.

A British regiment, the First-Fourth Norfolk, of several hundred men, was then noticed marching up this sunken road or creek towards Hill 60. However, when they arrived at this cloud, they marched straight into it, with no hesitation, but no one ever came out to deploy and fight at Hill 60. About an hour later, after the last of the file had disappeared into it, this cloud very unobtrusively lifted off the ground and, like any cloud or fog would, rose slowly until it joined the other similar clouds which were mentioned at the beginning of this account. On viewing them again, they all looked alike 'as peas in a pod'. All this time, the group of clouds had been hovering in the same place, but as soon as the singular cloud had risen to their level, they all moved away northwards, i.e., towards Thrace [Bulgaria]. In a matter of about three-quarters of an hour they had all disappeared from view.

The regiment mentioned is posted as missing or 'wiped out' and on Turkey surrendering in 1918, the first thing Britain demanded of Turkey was the return of this regiment.

Turkey replied that she had neither captured this regiment, nor made contact with it, and did not know it existed. A British Regiment in 1914–18 consisted of any number between 800 and 4,000 men. Those who observed this incident vouch for the fact that Turkey never captured that regiment, nor made contact with it.

We, the undersigned, although late in time, this is the 50th Jubilee of the ANZAC landing, declare that the above described incident is true in every word.

Signed by witnesses:

4/165 Sapper F. Reichardt
Matata, Bay of Plenty
13/416 Sapper R. Newnes
157 King Street, Cambridge
J. L. Newman
75 Freyberg Street,
Octumoctai, Tauranga

This is a truly incredible story, so incredible, in fact, that one's initial reaction is to dismiss it as fabrication, particularly as it is at fault on one major fact; the First-Fourth Norfolk did *not* vanish. Mr Reichardt could not have witnessed the disappearance of the First-Fourth Norfolk, but he was looking back over fifty years when he told his story in 1965, so maybe he confused the details but was nevertheless honest and sincere in the main substance of his story; in which case we must ask ourselves if Reichardt and his comrades *did* witness the event described and, if so, could the troops involved have been the remnants of the First-Fifth Norfolk.

If Reichardt was describing the fate of the First-Fifth Norfolk, his account contains many errors: he identified the wrong battalion and called it a regiment; he said that they were abducted on the morning of 21 August when marching towards Hill 60, but the First-Fifth's advance was in the afternoon of 12 August and Hill 60 was held by the enemy throughout that time and was at least three miles to the south of the location of the Norfolk's advance. A further small point: Reichardt, and all subsequent accounts, say the disappearance took place on Hill 60, Suvla Bay, ANZAC; ANZAC is not a place, it is an acronym for Australia and New Zealand Army Corps.

There seems little reason why we should believe Reichardt's story, and yet he was at Gallipoli (he was a sailor enlisted in the United Kingdom Section of the New Zealand Expeditionary Force on 8 October 1914, as a member of No 3 Section, 1st Divisional Field Company, New Zealand Engineers, and he embarked for Gallipoli on 12 April 1915), so unless he fabricated his story, he must have seen or thought he saw something that afternoon over fifty years ago. Before progressing further, however, it would be helpful to refresh our memory of the appearance of Suvla. A semicircle of bleak hills runs from north to south and gives the plain the appearance of a giant natural arena. To the south is Sari Bair – Turkish for the 'yellow ridge' – which has three summits, all about 1,000 feet in height, separated from each other by about half a mile of undulating crest line. The northernmost peak is Koja Chemen Tepe, the next is Besim Tepe, known to the British as Hill Q, and the third, 850 feet high, is Chunuk Bair. One and a half miles to the north of Chunuk Bair is a small hillock called Hill 60, and a further three miles to the north is Kuchuk Anafarta Ova, where the First-Fifth Norfolk advanced on 12 August.

The most practical route to the summit of Chunuk Bair is along a spur which the Allies called the Rhododendron Spur because of the red flowers (not actually rhododendrons) that blazed along its length during the early days of the campaign. It was from the Rhododendron Spur that Reichardt claims to have seen the British troops abducted by a cloud.

According to the *War Diary* of the 1st Divisional Field Company (War History WA 61/1, National Archives, Wellington, New Zealand, No 3 Section was well-digging away from the Rhododendron Spur until 13 August 1915. On that date the *War Diary* records: 'Work continued by Nos 1, 2, and 4 Sections, No 3 being transferred to new positions on Rhododendron Spur for similar class of work on trenches, communications, gun emplacements, and general Engineers' work in consolidating and improving position.' Therefore, if the *War Diary* is correct, Reichardt and his company were not entrenched on the Spur on 12 August, when the First-Fifth vanished. However, it is possible that No 3 Section was moved up to the Spur during the afternoon of the 12th in order to begin work there at dawn the following day, and the officer writing up the diary might have omitted to record this.

It is possible, though unlikely, that, disorientated after the fighting, the First-Fifth became lost and blindly wandered around Suvla Plain for nine days. If Reichardt's date of the 21st is accurate, then it surely cannot have been the First-Fifth whose fate he witnessed. However, 21 is the reverse of 12, so could he have got the numbers mixed? If so, and assuming that the *War Diary* is inaccurate and No 3 Section was moved to the Rhododendron Spur during the afternoon of the 12th, Reichardt might have had an unimpeded view of the low ground to the north, where the Norfolks were operating, but whether or not he could accurately observe what was happening is another matter. Reichardt and his Company were at least four and a half miles from the scene of the Norfolk's advance and his powers of observation must have indeed been acute if he could see what was happening over such a distance and in the battle conditions pertaining.

I don't believe that the men of No 3 Section could have seen much over such a distance and I don't believe that the Section witnessed the fate of the First-Fifth Norfolk. The details of Reichardt's story, whether they be applied to the First-Fourth or to the First-Fifth, are in error, and if the details are wrong, why should we believe the main substance of his tale? Yet, unless his story is a complete and utter fabrication, he must have seen something and later confused what he had seen (or perhaps only heard about) with the disappearance of the First-Fifth. But *what* did he see? What caused the confusion?

Some versions of Reichardt's story contain mention of a record of the abduction in one of the official histories of the Gallipoli Campaign: 'They were swallowed up by an unseasonable fog. This fog reflected the sun's rays in such a manner that artillery observers were dazzled by its brilliance and were unable to fire in support. The two hundred and fifty men were never seen or heard from again.'

Such an entry in an official history of the Campaign would, of course, shed a different light on the veracity of Reichardt's story, but none of the official reports consulted by or on behalf of the present writer contain such an entry. However, referring back to *The Final Report Of The Dardanelles Commission* mentioned earlier, we find the following entry on the page facing the account of the Norfolk's advance: 'By some freak of nature Suvla Bay and Plain were wrapped in a strange mist . . . We had reckoned on the enemy's gunners being blinded by the declining sun.' This entry bears such a striking resemblance to the entry in Reichardt's 'official history' that it is difficult not to believe that they are one and the same. Moreover, the entry refers to an event which took place on 21 August, the date given by Reichardt, when an unseasonable but perfectly normal mist descended shortly after noon and wrought havoc with what was the greatest offensive, in terms of numbers, launched at Gallipoli. During that afternoon a composite ANZAC force of 3,000 men attacked Hill 60 and a battle raged there for almost a week before the Allies abandoned the corpse-strewn hillock to the Turks. Not far from Hill 60 another attack was launched against Scimitar Hill, a low, rounded Spur which juts out into Suvla Bay. It was here, shortly before dusk, that Sir John Milbanke, VC, a friend of Winston Churchill, led the Sherwood Rangers against the enemy. They charged into the evil, swirling gloom of that unseasonable mist and were lost to sight. The Turks, positioned above the mist, were ideally situated, however, and destroyed the Sherwood Rangers.

Is it possible that Reichardt, telling his story after fifty years, confused the disappearance of the First-Fifth Norfolk with the unseasonable mist and the destruction of the Sherwood Rangers? I believe that he did. It is significant that both events were on facing pages in *The Final Report* and that the *Report* was declassified in 1965, the year that Reichardt told his story.

And, while on the subject of Reichardt telling his story, it is interesting to trace how the tale came into being in the first place. It was first told on 25 August 1965 at an old comrades-at-arms reunion to celebrate the 50th Jubilee of the ANZAC landing. It was later printed in the September 1965 issue of the New Zealand journal *Spaceview* and in the March 1966 issue of an American UFO magazine, *Flying Saucers*. Since then the story of the 'kidnapping cloud' has been told time and again, principally by writers involved with the UFO enigma, among them notables such as Charles Berlitz, Ralph Blum, John Keel, Brad Steiger, Brinsley Le Poer Trench and Jacques Vallée, to name but a few. Sad to say, not a single one of them would appear to have done any research or made any attempt to verify Reichardt's story.

However, if you accept my theory about Reichardt's confusion, we are still left with a mystery. What *did* happen to the missing Norfolks? Well, at least two, Captain Coxon and Lieutenant C. S. Fawkes, were captured and taken prisoner, spending the rest of the war in captivity in Asia Minor, from where they were eventually repatriated. Other Norfolks no doubt similarly suffered and many were probably wounded. Turkish prison camps were notorious for their poor conditions, so it is quite likely that many sick and wounded men died in captivity. Others were probably killed in the advance. Care of the dead was rudimentary and bodies are still being found on the battlefield today. And, strange as it may seem, some of the missing Norfolks were probably never missing at all, but were among those who became separated during the advance, returning to camp after nightfall.

In the final analysis, however, we don't know for certain what fate befell those men, but, in time of war, men and women disappear in their thousands. The Commonwealth War Graves Commission's memorials around the world bear the names of 771,982 Commonwealth dead of the two World Wars who have no known grave. These memorials, mostly located in theatres of war where the casualties were highest, range in size from small tablets bearing a few names to majestic monuments bearing many thousands of names. For example, the Thiepval Memorial to the missing of the Somme bears 72,073 names and the Menin Gate Memorial to the missing of Ypres Salient bears 54,360 names. In light of figures such as these the disappearance of less than 150 men from one of the most bloody and hellish battlefields in modern history cannot be considered unusual.

6 The Phantoms, the Derelicts and the Haunted

Some ships seem to possess a personality of their own that remains unchanged no matter what man may do to try to change them. There are good ships and bad ships; some ships seem cursed by misfortune and others damned by evil; others haunt and some are haunted; some disappear and others are found inexplicably deserted.

Mary Celeste (see pages 88–117) was by no means the first vessel found drifting aimlessly without her crew. *Rosalie* pre-dates *Mary Celeste* by several decades. The following item appeared on page six of *The Times* for Friday, 6 November 1840:

SHIP DESERTED – A letter from Nassau in the Bahamas, bearing the date 27th of August, has the following narrative: a singular fact has taken place within the last few days. A large French vessel, bound from Hamburgh to Havanah, was met by one of our coasters, and was discovered to be completely abandoned. The greater part of her sails were set, and she did not seem to have sustained any damage. The cargo, composed of wines, fruits, silks, etc., was in the most perfect condition. The captain's papers were all secure in their proper places. The soundings gave three feet of water in the hold, but there was no leak whatsoever. The only living things on board were a cat, some fowles, and several canaries half-dead with hunger. The cabins of the officers and passengers were very elegantly furnished, and everything indicated that they had only recently been deserted. In one of them were found several articles belonging to a ladies toilet together with a quantity of ladies wearing apparel thrown hastily aside, but not a human being was to be found on board. The vessel, which must have been left within a very few hours, contained several bales of goods addressed to different merchants in Havanah. She is very large, recently built, and called *Rosalie*. Of her crew and passengers no intelligence has been received.

The Times carried no further information about *Rosalie* and inquiries with Lloyd's of London and the Musée de la Marine in Paris have failed to produce any new material. Indeed, the most diligent research has not uncovered any data about *Rosalie* beyond that which is given in *The Times* article. However, I have unearthed a vessel called *Rossini* which may be the key to the mystery.

Lloyd's record that on 3 August 1840 a vessel called *Rossini* ran aground on the Muares (the Bahama Channel) *en route* to Havana from Hamburg. Her passengers and crew were rescued and taken to safety. Two weeks later, on 17 August, the British wrecking ships *Resolute* and *Seaflower* under the command of Benjamin Curry and John Baptiste salvaged *Rossini* and took her to Nassau, where they filed a claim for salvage. The salvage hearing was held in the Vice Admiralty Court; in the Minutes (1837–1842 SC4/8) mention is made of an affadavit presented by Curry and Baptiste testifying to 'curious circumstances' under which the vessel had been found. Unfortunately, this affadavit seems to have been lost and no mention of the precise nature of the 'curious circumstances' is made in surviving documents relating to the case. Is it possible that the phrase might mean that neither the salvagers nor the authorities in Nassau were aware that *Rossini* had run aground two weeks earlier and that her passengers and crew had been taken to safety?

There are similarities between the two ships: they were found in the same general area and in the same month of the same year; they were both bound from Hamburg to Havana; and their names, *Rosalie* and *Rossini*, are similar enough to have been mistaken for one another. However, there are differences, too. The *Rossini*'s passengers were taken to safety on 3 August: two weeks later, on 17 August, the ship was salvaged. The *Rosalie* story in *The Times* was from a dispatch dated Nassau, 27 August, some ten days after *Rossini* had been brought into port and twenty-four days after her passengers and crew had been rescued. Now, if *Rosalie* and *Rossini* are one and the same, the ship would have been abandoned for up to twenty-four days, which does not tally with *The Times*' statement that 'the vessel must have been left within a very few hours'. On the other hand, *The Times* article does tend to contradict itself when it says that a cat, some 'fowles' and canaries found aboard the ship were half-dead with hunger. This fact would seem to suggest that the ship had been deserted for more than a few hours.

The question of *Rosalie/Rossini* remains unresolved, yet it does not seem unlikely that the Editor of *The Times* or the newspaper's Nassau correspondent misspelled or misread *Rossini* and called the ship *Rosalie*. But if this was not the case – what a mystery!

One overcast morning in 1850 fishermen and residents of Easton's Beach, near Newport, Rhode Island, saw a large ship heading toward dangerous coral reefs not far from shore. The sea was rough and the vessel was under full sail, a strong wind driving her forward. It was evident that she was going to run aground, but shout and wave as they would, the residents of Easton's Beach could not attract the attention of anyone on board.

The vessel sped onward and, to everybody's astonishment, by some miracle avoided the reefs – only to be presented with a new danger; it would surely come to grief on the shore, perhaps with a considerable loss of life. The wind filled her sails and drove her onward. Then, when disaster seemed inevitable, a huge wave appeared from nowhere, caught the ship under the bow and lifted her onto the beach, where she sank into the soft, wet sand.

The fishermen hauled themselves over the vessel's side and dropped to the deck. A mongrel dog sat there and surveyed them with calm, untroubled eyes. The dog was the only living thing on board. A search of the ship revealed it to be otherwise deserted. However, there was ample evidence that the ship had been fully manned until recently: there was a pot of coffee boiling on the galley stove; the galley table was laid with plates and cutlery in preparation for breakfast; and a distinct aroma of fresh tobacco smoke lingered in the air. Papers identified the ship as *Seabird* under the command of John Huxham (some accounts say John Durham), bound from the Honduras for her home port of Newport. The log contained a recent entry, the sighting of Brenton's Reef a few miles off-shore. Somebody suggested that *Seabird*'s crew had abandoned ship in fear that their vessel was about to be torn to shreds on the reef and this was the generally accepted theory until the crew of a fishing boat reported having exchanged signals with the *Seabird* shortly after the vessel had passed the reef and when all danger was passed. Nevertheless, residents of Easton's Beach kept alert for any news of survivors or bodies being found along the shore – but none ever were.

Seabird's cargo – dye-woods, hardwoods, pitch-pine and coffee – was unloaded and carried by wagons to Newport, where it was delivered to its owners. As for *Seabird*, she was stuck in the sand and several attempts to shift her failed. She was finally left to sink into the wet sand.

Not long after the vessel's arrival a violent storm swept Easton's Beach. Ferocious winds whipped up mountainous waves and sent them crashing over the beach with explosive force. *Seabird* would be matchwood by morning, or so the locals thought – but the next day, when they ventured down to the sands, they found nothing. *Seabird* had vanished and there was no trace of her, not even a tiny scrap of wreckage. She had gone back to sea!

Nobody could offer a sensible explanation and the authorities were baffled, but it was whispered in the local bars that *Seabird* was a real ghost ship – a vessel truly crewed by ghosts – and that her company had gone back to sea after a ghostly shore-leave.

Many accounts of this story say that the people of Easton's Beach found the mystery on their doorstep beyond belief. I also find it beyond belief: by what miracle did a pot of boiling coffee stay on the galley stove throughout the vessel's stormy arrival? Would a dog have been calmly sitting on deck instead of cowering in some corner after that tempestuous journey? I don't find this story credible and I can't find any contemporary sources. The earliest source for this tale of 1850 that I can find is *Forgotten Mysteries* by R. DeWitt Miller published in 1947.

On 28 February 1855, *Marathon* sighted a bark about six hundred miles from the Azores (about 30° N, 40° W). It 'was yawing back and forth and appeared to be sailing with no one at the wheel', reported *Marathon*'s skipper.

A boarding party crossed to the vessel, which was called *James B. Chester*, and found her deserted, although evidence suggested a hurried evacuation: chairs and tables had been knocked over and drawers had been pulled out and their contents scattered over the deck. But there were no signs of bloodshed and it was discovered that the compass and ship's papers were missing, indications that the ship had been evacuated. But the strange thing about *James B. Chester* was that all the lifeboats were hanging in the davits.

Marathon's skipper put a skeleton crew aboard *Chester* and the vessel eventually arrived in Albert Docks, Liverpool, where a large crowd had gathered to see her arrival.

Nobody knows why *Chester*'s crew abandoned ship. The vessel was in excellent condition and her cargo was intact. The only explanation was that the crew had been taken aboard another ship (perhaps forcibly) – but for what reason? Or had the crew gone mad, the last man, the lone survivor of whatever malady befell them, having thrown the bodies over the side before casting himself into the ocean? Nobody knows what happened. Then, as now, all people could do was to look at the facts and speculate.

Iron Mountain was one of the largest Mississippi riverboats of her kind, in excess of 180 feet long, 35 feet across the beam and powered by five boilers. In June 1872 she left the city of Vicksburg with fifty-two passengers, a cargo of cotton bales tied to the deck and a string of barges carrying cotton and molasses towed astern. Sometime later the riverboat *Iroquois Chief* rounded a bend in the river just beyond Vicksburg and almost collided with a string of barges. Nobody was exceptionally alarmed: it was not uncommon for the tow-rope between a riverboat and her barges to slip free or snap, and the narrowness of the river made it impossible for the riverboat to turn and retrieve the barges. Nobody thought much about the incident until it was noticed that the tow-rope had been deliberately cut, an act committed only when a riverboat is in desperate trouble and fighting for her life.

It was subsequently learned that the abandoned barges belonged to *Iron Mountain*, and inquiries revealed that the riverboat had failed to arrive at her next port of call. Indeed, it was later confirmed that nobody had seen the vessel after she had rounded the bend in the river. A search of the area failed to find any wreckage, which was unusual: a fire or an explosion would have littered the river with debris for miles; had *Iron Mountain* sunk, her deck cargo of cotton bales would have been found floating in the river. But there was nothing.

Over the last century fishermen and visitors to that part of the Mississippi where *Iron Mountain* is alleged to have vanished have from time to time claimed that a ghostly voice could be heard coming from the middle of the river. Those who have heard it claim that the voice cries: '*Gaston! Gaston! Aides moi au nom de Dieu. Ces hommes me blessant!*' (Gaston! Gaston! Help me in the name of God. These men are hurting me!) Some people believe that the voice is that of a passenger aboard *Iron Mountain* and suggest (by some mystical reason beyond me) that it is evidence that the riverboat was hijacked, driven inshore, dismantled and the pieces carried away for reassembly elsewhere.

The story of *Ellen Austin* is a strange one and it will soon become apparent why a note on the sources is required before progressing further. The earliest source I have traced is the book *The Stargazer Talks*, a slim volume by Lt-Commander Rupert T. Gould,* where she is mentioned very briefly (10 lines/85 words) in a chapter about *Mary Celeste*, the subject of a radio broadcast by the author in 1935. Gould does not give his source, but he was an able, intelligent and objective researcher: there is no reason to believe that he would have invented the tale. However, there are several versions which differ from one another, the details of which I give here in case one of the sources goes beyond Gould – who, by the way, gives none of the dates mentioned other than 1881 and mentions no names except that of the ship.

One afternoon (some accounts say the afternoon of 14 July) in 1881 the lookout aboard the British (or American)

**The Stargazer Talks*, published in 1943, was based on a series of talks Gould gave for *Children's Hour*, a now long-defunct but fondly remembered sixty minutes of early-evening entertainment for children on BBC Radio.

schooner (or brig) *Ellen Austin*, becalmed in mid-Atlantic, sighted a twin-masted schooner off the starboard bow. *Ellen Austin*'s skipper, a man named Baker, surveyed the schooner through his telescope. The stranger was not flying a flag, the tailboards bearing the vessel's name were missing and there didn't seem to be anybody on board. Over the next few days the vessels drifted closer together and in the mid-afternoon (of 20 July) they were near enough for Baker to consider lowering a boat and taking a closer look at the stranger. With a crew of two (or four) Baker rowed across to the stranger and pulled himself over the side. The stranger's cargo was intact and secure, she was in seaworthy condition, and all her lifeboats secure in the davits – yet there was not a soul aboard.

Baker put a skeleton crew aboard and instructed them to follow *Ellen Austin* to St John's, Newfoundland (Gould says St John's, but other accounts variously state that *Ellen Austin* had been bound for Boston but had been forced to divert to St John's by bad weather; another account says that the vessel was bound for New York), where Baker planned to claim her as salvage, as soon as the winds picked up.

Two days later *Ellen Austin* and her prize found themselves in the grip of a violent storm. To the southeast the eastern Bahamas were being blasted by a howling fury, a hurricane that would spread destruction through Georgia, Alabama and Mississippi, claiming 700 lives before abating. For two days the storm raged around *Ellen Austin* and her unnamed prize and, when the skies eventually cleared, Baker and his men scanned the horizon seeking the salvage – but she had disappeared. Baker spent some time searching for the mystery schooner before dwindling supplies forced him to head for port.

Commander Gould and other tellers of the tale end their account here, but some continue, saying that, when the storm abated, those aboard *Ellen Austin* called to their shipmates aboard the schooner (which had not disappeared, according to these accounts) but were greeted by silence. With a feeling that history was repeating itself, Captain Baker boarded the schooner, finding her deserted. His skeleton crew had left the supplies untouched and disappeared without leaving any sign that they had ever been on board.

The men were unwilling to form another skeleton crew until

Baker dangled a sizeable financial carrot and thereby obtained several volunteers. He armed them with muskets and told them to keep the schooner within hailing distance. They were told to ring the mystery schooner's bell every quarter-hour and to abandon ship at the first hint of any trouble. In this manner the two vessels continued their voyage until (4 August or sometime in September) a thick mist enveloped the two ships. The crew of *Ellen Austin* shouted encouraging words to their comrades hidden behind an impenetrable blanket of grey fog, and the skeleton crew replied and rang the schooner's bell every quarter-hour – until that faint, reassuring sound came no more. When the mist lifted the schooner and the men on board had vanished, never to be seen again.

There is a rational explanation for what happened. The mystery schooner may have been in port, loaded with her cargo and awaiting propitious tides, when a sudden storm sprang up. The vessel was wrenched from her moorings and swept out to sea. Thus we could explain the absence of the crew and the presence of all the boats secure in their davits. As for the first skeleton crew: finding themselves fighting a ferocious storm, they may have decided to abandon ship and were drowned – or maybe they were washed overboard. The second skeleton crew, if there was one, may have abandoned ship, too, but it is more likely that they sailed away from *Ellen Austin* and became lost.

Marlborough was a wool clipper carrying a cargo of gold bullion, perhaps as much as $2,000,000 worth, which left New Zealand for England in 1890. She sailed from port and was never seen again. Nobody knows what fate befell her, but over the years many people have reported actually seeing her! One rumour says that she is ice-bound near the south pole. Another, and by far the most interesting, comes from the crew of the British ship *Johnson* who sighted an abandoned vessel off the coast of Chile in 1913. The derelict's sails were hanging in shreds and covered with some kind of green mould. A boarding party reported that her timbers were dangerously rotten and that the vessel's crew were all dead – six skeletons were found on the bridge, ten more were in the crew's quarters and several others were found scattered around the ship. On the prow, in faded letter, was the name – *Marlborough*.

My source for this incredible tale is *Invisible Horizons* by Vincent Gaddis, but his source seems to be a sober enough article in the *Evening Post* (Wellington, New Zealand) of 13 November 1913. Neither Gaddis nor the newspaper mention the cargo of gold. Was it still aboard? Had *Marlborough* been pirated? We shall never know. Nor will we ever learn how *Marlborough* survived the savage seas for twenty-three years, if indeed she did.

In October 1917 *Zebrina* left Falmouth, Cornwall, for St Brieux, France. Two days later, after reasonable weather, she was found deserted, in excellent condition, bearing no clues to suggest the fate of her crew. As in other cases before it, the *Zebrina*'s crew had vanished without trace. No explanation is evident.

In July 1941 the Portuguese lugger *Islandia*, a Red Cross charter vessel commanded by Captain Amadio Mathias, found the French cutter *Belle Isle* drifting near the Gulf of Lyon. She was in good condition, seaworthy, her sails were set and there was no sign of violence, yet there was nobody on board. The *Belle Isle* had been unaccountably abandoned.

This is one of the most recent such inexplicable mysteries. Certainly there must be others even more recent . . .

7 The Bermuda Triangle in Fantasy and Fact

Possibly the most alarming mystery to emerge in recent years is that of the Bermuda Triangle, a stretch of water confined within an imaginary triangle connecting Bermuda with the coast of Florida and the island of Puerto Rico, where a frighteningly high number of ships and aircraft are said to have disappeared without trace. What makes this mystery alarming, even more alarming than claims of an imminent UFO invasion, is the allegation that the disappearances are caused by a supernatural force which is beyond Man's understanding. In other words, a trip to Bermuda could cost you your life!

Several very popular books have been written about the Bermuda Triangle, each providing a wealth of evidence to back the authors' claims and theories, but how accurate is their evidence? Is there really a force causing ships and aircraft to vanish, or has the whole Bermuda Triangle mystery grown around misinterpretations and misstatements? In this chapter we shall examine the Bermuda Triangle, beginning with the popular story and concluding with an analysis of the 'evidence'.

Strange phenomena have been reported in the region since the days of Christopher Columbus.

Columbus sailed from the Canary Islands with three small ships – *Nina, Pinta* and *Santa Maria* – and ninety men. On the forty-third day of the voyage, Friday, 13 September 1492, Columbus noticed that the compass needle no longer pointed directly towards the North Star but instead about six degrees to the northwest; as the days passed, Columbus watched the compass needle move further and further from the North Star. Two days later Columbus and his men saw patches of seaweed,

which they took to be an indication of approaching land. No
land appeared, however, and Columbus' men grew increasingly
anxious. The seaweed ocean, the strange Sargasso Sea which
later romancers would weave into elaborate fantasies, was
followed by an even more wonderous phenomenon. A 'great
flame of fire', as Columbus described it, was seen to fall into
the sea. Nobody seems to have been alarmed and it was
believed to have been a meteor, but modern mariners have
reported similar fireballs in the Bermuda Triangle and their
descriptions, although similar to Columbus', do not fit meteors.

At about midnight on 11 October, Columbus was gazing
out to sea when he saw – or thought he saw – a light on the
horizon. He called for a fellow seaman, who also saw the
strange light. A third man was summoned, but the light had
gone by the time he arrived. A few hours later, Rodrigo de
Triana aboard the *Pinta* cried, 'Tierra! Tierra!' – Land!
Land! Landfall was made on a small island inhabited by a
friendly people whom Columbus called *los Indios* and made
immediate preparations to enslave.

Nobody knows on which of the many small Caribbean
islands Columbus made landfall. He called it San Salvador
and the general consensus of opinion seems to favour Watling
Island in the central Bahamas. But the big mystery is the
strange light Columbus saw shortly before landfall. What he
saw or could have seen is unknown and the light is one of the
earliest mysteries of the Bermuda Triangle.

Bermuda itself has long inspired superstition. Comprising
over three hundred islands, of which only about twenty are
inhabited, the Bermudas lie at the apex of the Triangle and
cover an area of twenty-one square miles, connected by bridges
and causeways to form an arc. Historians credit their discovery
to a Spaniard, Juan de Bermudez, who was stranded there in
1515, but there is some slight evidence to suggest that they
could have been discovered about one thousand years before
Columbus by an Irish monk named Brendan, known as 'The
Navigator' or 'The Voyager', one of the great Irish saints,
revered almost as highly as Brigid and only slightly less than
Patrick. He lived from about 489 to 570/83 and is credited
with many travels. His supposed voyage to the West Indies
and, indeed, to North America itself, is recorded in the
Navigatio Sancti Brendani Abbatis (The Voyage of St Brendan

the Abbot), of which there are at least one hundred and twenty Latin manuscripts in existence and more in other languages. The age of the earliest manuscript is conservatively estimated as the tenth century, but this is merely the time at which the manuscript was written down: the actual composition is believed to date from much earlier, perhaps as early as the ninth century. One eminent Celticist, Professor James Carney of the Dublin Institute of Advanced Studies, believes it was produced in Latin around 800AD! Although 800AD is two hundred years after Brendan's death, the date of 800–900AD is significant. Few scholars now dispute that Vikings reached America about 1000AD, and therefore any reference to America in documents after that date could be based on Norse sources; but, if the *Navigatio* were composed about 900AD or earlier, and if it does contain references to America, then its author must have had access to a pre-Viking account of a voyage to America.

According to the *Navigatio*, St Brendan and seventeen intrepid monks left Ireland in search of an island paradise where they could live in peace and silence. They returned after an absence of seven years and told of their many strange and wonderful adventures, one of which involved an island, possibly Bermuda, where at dusk the birds spoke to them. Brendan thought that the birds were harbingers of heaven, and called the island the 'Isle of the Blest'.

In the 1600s Captain Diego Ramirez, skipper of a 750-ton galleon called *San Domingo*, was stranded on Bermuda when a severe storm forced *San Domingo* aground on a pocket of sand in quiet waters which are known today as Spanish Point. A few repairs necessitated a lengthy stay on the island; and, on his return home, Ramirez wrote an account and drew a map of the islands – the earliest known map of Bermuda. Both remained in the Archives of the Indies in Seville for three hundred and fifty years until they were found and translated by Lawrence Gurrin, the late archivist of Bermuda.

According to Ramirez, on the first night of their stay he and his men were terrified by the 'devils' of Bermuda. At dusk there was a terrible shrieking and cries that sounded like somebody shouting 'tell 'em, tell 'em'. Ramirez told his men, '. . . these are the devils of Bermuda which they say are here-abouts', and he advised them to make the sign of the cross.

At the time of this disturbance a luckless crewman, a negro named Venturilla, was ashore, cutting a piece of cedar to replace the broken rudder of a small boat. He was suddenly heard to call for help, then the still evening air was rent by a horrible scream. He was found dead, apparently attacked and overwhelmed by birds attracted by the light of his lantern. Those same birds were also responsible for the shrieking and cries which had so frightened Ramirez and his men. They were cahows, a species thought to be extinct until a few pairs were found nesting in the caves of Castle Island, Bermuda, in 1950. The cahows begin an incessant chatter about dusk, which is the time when Ramirez and his men were frightened by the 'devils' and when the birds on the 'Isle of the Blest' spoke to St Brendan, a coincidence which has led some people to speculate that the 'Isle of the Blest' is Bermuda.

Interestingly, by Ramirez's time the Bermudas had an established reputation as a place of devils, yet can the simple cry of a bird have instilled fear into the hearts of hard-bitten seafarers? Were the cahows responsible for Bermuda's unsavoury reputation? Surely there must be a deeper reason; the islands have an equable climate, there is plenty of food and fresh water, and to the early American colonists who were used to a hard and bitter struggle for survival it should have seemed like paradise, yet the islands were shunned and so disliked that they remained uninhabited for almost a century after their discovery.

Despite the undoubted fact that the Spanish would have made good use of Bermuda as a mid-ocean refuge and provisioning base, it was not until 1609, when the *Sea Venture*, a sturdy, full-rigged British galleon carrying one hundred and fifty emigrants from England to Virginia, was wrecked there that men first began to colonise the lonely islands.

One of a flotilla of vessels which sailed from Plymouth Harbour for the Jamestown Colony in Virginia on 2 June 1609, the *Sea Venture* was the flagship of Sir George Somers and under the command of Christopher Newport. Among the passengers was the newly appointed Lieutenant-Governor of Jamestown, Sir Thomas Gates. On 23 June the flotilla was separated by a hurricane. The storm grew worse as the days passed and the *Sea Venture* sprang a leak. Sir Thomas Gates' secretary, a man named William Strachey, wrote that many times he gave up hope of ever reaching land and often wondered at the futility of continuing to battle against destiny. 'Why should we labour to preserve life?' he wrote. 'Yet we did, either because so dear are a few lingering hours of life or because our Christian knowledge taught us . . . not to neglect the means of our own preservation . . .'

Strachey recorded that on Friday, 29 July, 'when morning was three-quarters spent and when no one dreamed of salvation, Sir George Somers, peering through the curtain of fine rain, described land'. Coincidentally, as land had been heralded by the strange lights seen by Columbus, so it was for those aboard the *Sea Venture*. Strachey wrote that on the previous night Sir George Somers had seen 'a little round light like a fair star, trembling and streaming along with a sparkling blaze, half the height upon the main mast, and shooting sometimes from shroud to shroud, tempting to settle as it were upon any of the four shrouds: as for three or four hours together, or rather more, half the night, it kept with us running sometimes along the mainyard to the very end and then returning'.

The *Sea Venture* was beyond repair and Captain Newport attempted to beach her near the shore, but her hull grounded between two rocks on a reef about three-quarters of a mile from the shore. By late afternoon, as a fitful sun tried to break through the clouds, the ship's company, including the ship's dog, was safe on the white sands of Bermuda.

The following days were spent stripping the *Sea Venture* of all that was salvable, including the timbers from which it was hoped to build a pinnace. Finally, nothing remained of the *Sea Venture* beyond her stark ribcage; then it, too, vanished.

The colonists' first task was to convert the *Sea Venture's* longboat for a voyage to Virginia to obtain help from the Jamestown colonists. On 28 August one of Sir George Somers' best men, a master's mate and good pilot named Henry Ravens, set off for Virginia with a crew of six. They never returned.

The passengers and crew of the *Sea Venture* finally left Bermuda in two pinnaces they had built and reached Jamestown, where they were met by a handful of ragged, half-starved creatures, the remains of the four-hundred-and-fifty-strong colony. The winter had been hard and the food short. Only sixty colonists had survived.

(In October 1958 a SCUBA diving enthusiast named Edmund

Downing was swimming off the southeast coast of Bermuda, appropriately enough near Sea Venture Shoal, when he saw a ship's hull outlined on the sand bottom. The authorities investigated and after expert opinion had been sought it was announced that Downing had found the remains of the *Sea Venture*.)

The wreck of the *Sea Venture* inspired *The Tempest*, William Shakespeare's last complete play and perhaps his finest. Devotees of the Bermuda Triangle claim that a line in *The Tempest* – 'From the still-vexed Bermooths' – is a reference to the supernatural forces operating in the region. It more likely refers to the dangerous coral reefs which surround the Bermudas and which claimed almost a hundred Elizabethan vessels, but it is argued that 'vexed' is a strange adjective to describe disaster-ridden reefs. In return one might argue that it is an equally odd word with which to describe an undefined supernatural force.

However, something must have given Bermuda its evil reputation. The cahows seem unlikely to have struck fear into tough, albeit superstitious, seamen for so long; and the Bahamas and Straits of Florida claimed more ships than the reefs of Bermuda, yet did not gain an evil reputation. Perhaps the only realistic explanation is that then, as today, Bermuda was associated with unaccountable disappearances, fair-weather shipwrecks, inexplicably abandoned ships and odd phenomena like strange lights and balls of fire.

Ships have been vanishing in the Bermuda Triangle for hundreds of years, but nobody seems to have paid much attention to the high incidence of losses until 1945, when Flight 19, five US Navy bombers, vanished after sending a series of 'inexplicable' radio messages (see page 128); the mystery was heightened when a flying boat involved in the search reached the last known location of the bombers and followed them into oblivion. As one might expect, the six aircraft lost in one afternoon provoked considerable interest and many people began to take a close look at the region. Researchers compiled a disturbing list of unexplained disappearances that stretched back over one hundred years; taken individually each case looked no more than a tragic accident, but viewed as a whole they suggested that ships and aircraft

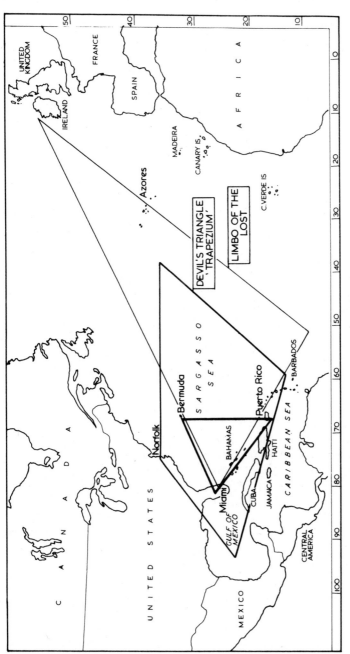

Although the Bermuda Triangle is generally shown as an imaginary triangle connecting Bermuda, Florida and Puerto Rico, several writers conceive it as encompassing larger areas of ocean. To some it is almost half the size of the North Atlantic, which is by no means small.

had vanished – and were continuing to vanish – in such numbers that no rational explanation was possible. As researcher and writer Ivan T. Sanderson put it in his book *Invisible Residents*, 'the number of disappearances is out of all proportion to such recorded losses elsewhere'.

The area where the majority of losses occurred was given many names – 'Devil's Triangle', 'Limbo of the Lost', 'Hoodoo Sea', 'Point of No Return', 'Pentagon of Death', 'Triangle of Tragedy', 'Port of the Missing', and 'Magic Rhombus' to name but a few – but the region has become known worldwide as the Bermuda Triangle, a name coined by Vincent Gaddis for an article entitled 'The Deadly Bermuda Triangle' which appeared in *Argosy* magazine in February 1964, being subsequently expanded for a chapter in Gaddis' book *Invisible Horizons*.

In fact the name 'Bermuda Triangle' is, as most researchers would now agree, a misnomer: Bermuda is not at the centre of the affected portion of ocean and the affected portion of ocean is not a triangle, although there is some dispute as to its actual shape and size. Author Richard Winer calls the region the Devil's Triangle, but maintains that it is a trapezium (see map), and adds that 'the first four letters of the word trapezium more than adequately describe it'. Another Triangle writer, John Wallace Spencer, calls the region the 'Limbo of the Lost' and visualises it as a scalene triangle – a triangle with no equal sides, whereas the Bermuda Triangle is depicted as roughly isosceles, having two sides of equal length – stretching from the Gulf of Mexico to the coast of South America, across almost to the coast of Ireland and back to the Gulf. Ivan T. Sanderson, however, calls the region a sort of 'funny blob, which extends from about $30°$ to $40°$ north latitude and about $55°$ to $85°$ west'. Whatever its actual size and shape, many people believe the Bermuda Triangle is a place where ships and aircraft vanish with appalling regularity, without explanation and in numbers far above what could be called average. Moreover, although once shy of publicity and adverse to talk about their experiences in the Bermuda Triangle, many seamen and pilots have told of weird experiences in the region: radio 'dead zones', compass needles unaccountably spinning madly, inexplicable breakdown of electrical power, strange objects seen in the sky and tracked in the depths of the ocean, and much more. Possibly the strangest phenomenon of all is what has been variously described as a yellow or green cloud or fog into which ships have sailed, never to be seen again.

The sky was clear and the weather good one afternoon in 1966 when the tug *Good News* suddenly found herself battling for life in the region of Tongue of the Ocean *en route* from Puerto Rico to Fort Lauderdale. A strange milky fog suddenly descended, the compass began spinning clockwise and all the electrical equipment ceased to function. The ship's generators were functioning but it was as if something were draining off the power; it was later discovered that fifty flashlight batteries and the tug's own batteries were dead. Don Henry, skipper of the *Good News* and owner of the Sea Phantom Exploration Company of Miami, rammed the throttles full ahead, and the tug inched forward, gradually slipping free of the 'fog'. Don Henry looked behind. The *Good News* had been towing a 2,500 ton barge astern on a thousand feet of line and, to Don Henry's amazement, he saw that only the barge was enveloped by the fog: everywhere else there was good visibility. The barge finally emerged and Don Henry headed for home. He didn't know what the 'fog' was and he didn't hang around to find out.

In June 1975 many American newspapers carried the story of two missionaries, Warren and Betty Miller, who flew into what they later described as a 'yellowish haze' when travelling from Guatemala to Key West, Florida. They had flown the route many times and knew it well, but in the vicinity of Cuba their 'plane's instruments went haywire. Warren Miller executed a 30° turn, putting the 'plane directly over Cuba – only Cuba wasn't there. Nothing existed below except a yellowish haze; for almost two hours the Millers floundered about in the haze, their instruments and radio dead, before finally emerging to find their equipment functioning normally again.

Many other strange phenomena have been described. Following the publication of extracts from Charles Berlitz's best-selling *The Bermuda Triangle* in the *Sunday Express* in 1975 several of the newspaper's readers wrote to tell of their own weird experiences. One correspondent described an unnerving experience which occurred just after dawn on a summer's day in 1955 when he was on lookout duty aboard *m/v Atlantic City*; the ship was on automatic steering and he was chatting to the mate when the ship suddenly began steering a circle, the gyrocompass and electrical equipment went dead and the binnacle compass began dancing in its bowl. At the same time a huge ball of fire – reminiscent of the one observed by Christopher Columbus – passed silently overhead, leaving a strange turbulence on the sea.

An even stranger thing happened to the Cunard liner *QE2* on a voyage in April 1974. According to Charles Berlitz, on 3 April, the liner's boilers suddenly and unaccountably failed, there was an interruption of electrical power and several other mechanical failures, and at the same time the liner's image disappeared from the radar screen of a nearby Coast Guard vessel, although the liner could still be seen by observers on the cutter's deck.

Radar malfunction (if malfunction it be) is common in the Bermuda Triangle. In August 1974, when returning to Miami from activities near Andros Island in the Bahamas, the Coast Guard cutter *Hollyhock* picked up a phantom landmass on radar. The radar was checked and no malfunction could be found, yet it still showed a landmass some ten miles distant. At the time the *Hollyhock* was some fifty miles from the Florida coast. The phantom remained ten miles ahead, moving at a uniform speed with the vessel, until it merged with the Florida mainland.

The *Hollyhock* seems to have run the gamut of weird experiences in the Bermuda Triangle. Off the north coast of Haiti in November 1974, the *Hollyhock*'s radio operator found himself unable to raise any local radio station, yet San Francisco, on the Pacific coast, came through loud and clear. On another occasion, when the *Hollyhock* was off Cuba, the radio operator could contact Mobile, Alabama, when all local stations were unaccountably dead.

The source of these stories is Lieutenant Bill Wissman. Interviewed on the BBC television documentary, *The Case For The Bermuda Triangle*, he stated that such phenomena were not uncommon and happened particularly at night when the atmospherics change. As for the phantom landmass, he said that sea conditions could look like land the further out on radar they get. However, Richard Winer, who describes the *Hollyhock*'s experiences in his book *The Devil's Triangle 2*, maintains that the cause of such phenomena is a mystery. The authorities know it happens and they know it's not particularly dangerous, he says, but they can't explain it and anything that cannot be explained is perforce a mystery.

The Bermuda Triangle is a mystery that many have attempted to solve. Another area with a high incidence of unaccountable losses was sought in the hope that it might provide a common denominator. One such area was found in the Pacific, off the coast of Japan; an area with a long history of unexplained disappearances and fair-weather shipwrecks, it had been the source of stories about sea monsters, the kraken, giant squid and other horrors of the depths for years, but only small fishing craft of doubtful stability had been lost and the authorities had remained unimpressed. Then, between 1950 and 1954, no less than nine large coastal freighters vanished in good weather and, with the exception of one case, when a vessel radioed the word 'sinking', none had sent an SOS. In each case no wreckage was found.

The Japanese authorities grew alarmed and, in 1955, sent a scientific expedition to investigate. To everyone's horror the *No. 5 Kaiyo Maru*, her crew and party of scientists, failed to return to port. The research vessel and all aboard had joined the legion of the missing in what is now known as the 'Devil's Sea'. As a result the authorities declared the region an official danger zone.

Writer Ivan T. Sanderson was one of the first to study the Devil's Sea and he wrote of the results of his research in his book *Invisible Residents*: 'The outcome was not just amazing, it was positively startling. Plane after plane on its way south to Guam appears to have vanished, and this with very disturbing frequency.'

But even more startling than his revelations about the Devil's Sea was Sanderson's discovery of what he believed numbered at least twelve anomalous regions, which he called Vile Vortices, encircling the globe. He wrote: 'Planes, ships, and subs have, as we have stressed, been disappearing all over the world. But it has to be admitted that many more are reported to have done so in these . . . areas than in any others.' Elsewhere in his book he wrote: 'The Services . . . know perfectly well that there is something "not right" about this, but they haven't got any more idea than we have as to what it could be.' Theories, however, are almost as legion as the disappearances, the favoured one being some kind of electro-magnetic anomaly.

Back in 1492 Columbus noticed that the compass needle moved away from the North Pole the further he sailed into the Bermuda Triangle. Today we know, as Columbus guessed, that the compass needle does not actually point directly to the North Pole but to a magnetic Pole some 1,300 miles from the actual. However, while the compass needle points to the magnetic North Pole everywhere else in the world, in the Bermuda Triangle and the Devil's Sea it points to the actual North Pole. This had led a number of people to believe that the disappearances are caused by an electromagnetic anomaly, a view which seems supported by the discoveries claimed by a Canadian named Wilbert B. Smith of the Telecommunications Division of the Canadian Department of Transport who, in December 1950, was authorised by the Deputy Minister of Transport for Air Services to undertake a study of the UFO phenomenon. Codenamed Project Magnet, Smith's investigation lasted until late 1954, when he issued a report. Therein he claimed to have found what he called 'areas of reduced binding', places about 1,000 feet in diameter which contained forces capable of literally tearing aircraft apart. But, most alarming, these areas either moved about or appeared and disappeared without known cause!

Inspired or perhaps alarmed by Smith's discoveries, the United States Navy launched their own Project Magnet. The results are unknown, but it is believed that one Navy patrol bomber found the answer – it vanished along with the sensitive magnetic anomaly detector it carried.

Numerous theories have been advanced. Ivan T. Sanderson suggested that the disappearances were connected with the first tentative examination of our species by a civilised lifeform that lives on the sea bed and which has grown alarmed by our technology which, if we are not careful, could destroy us and them. In 1973 Dr John Harder, Professor of Engineering at Berkeley and a UFO investigator, suggested that the Earth was some kind of cosmic zoo and that the losses were to do with some kind of sample check by the keepers. Another view is that the Bermuda Triangle is a kind of doorway into time, a rip in the timestream through which our ships and aircraft are diverted into the future or the past or into some kind of limbo where time flows quickly, slowly or not at all. A popular theory suggests that the Bermuda Triangle was the location of Atlantis, the legendary home of a super-race who destroyed themselves with their awesome weapons, their island sinking beneath the waves in a terrible holocaust which precipitated the Biblical Flood. One of their weapons, a sort of ray gun used to destroy the vessels of Atlantis' enemies, is still functioning, it is said, and destroying our vessels today.

UFO writer and researcher John A. Keel claims that UFOs regularly appear in specific areas, pursue a course within a two-hundred-mile radius, and disappear. One of the major areas, or windows, as Keel calls them, is in the Gulf of Mexico, part of the Limbo of the Lost. And another Triangle investigator named Art Ford has pointed out that the United States space-shot sector is in the Bermuda Triangle and suggests that the same reasons which make it a good place from which to launch rockets might also make it a good place to land UFOs. As for Triangle writer John Wallace Spencer, he is personally convinced that UFOs provide the only rational explanation for the Bermuda Triangle mystery.

Theories about the Bermuda Triangle abound and while talk of Atlantis, UFOs and cosmic zoos are certainly sensationalist, it cannot be denied that, if the stories of the disappearances are being accurately told, then the Bermuda Triangle is a mystery for which science has no answer. Why then has the region remained the province of 'UFO' writers and not been seriously investigated?

To begin with, the so-called Bermuda Triangle is only a small area of water in comparison to the Atlantic Ocean. Triangle writers disagree about the region's precise size and shape, but at its largest it is about half the size of the North Atlantic Ocean and at its smallest it is about the size of the United Kingdom. It is also very busy; something in the region of 150,000 boats cross the area every year and it would be safe to say that day and night the region is being crossed by military, commercial and private aircraft, ships and boats.

The Bermuda Triangle is also a rather unique patch of ocean. Here the Gulf Stream, a fast-moving body of water, flows north at a steady four knots – just under five miles an hour – sufficient to carry an unwary or careless boater miles off course in a matter of hours or to sweep wreckage or debris far from the search area. The Triangle region is also noted for severe storms that can break without warning, for hurricanes, waterspouts, and virtually the whole of Nature's armoury, including freak seas caused by the changing topography of the sea bed or submarine volcanic activity; the former causes what is known as an impulsively generated or *seich* wave which can appear without warning and is not easy to see. *Seich* waves have been known to send a ship to the bottom in a matter of minutes, but they are mere infants in comparison to the awesome tsunami, gigantic salt-water Everests several hundred feet high caused by a submarine landslide or volcanic activity.

As for the disappearances: the Seventh District Coastguard, headquartered in Miami, which has jurisdiction over the Bermuda Triangle, is one of the busiest stations in the world and receives about 10,000 calls for help every year. This figure may seem high until compared to the number of boats in the region – 150,000 – and dwindles almost to insignificance when you realise that, on average, only about one hundred vessels are lost annually. Indeed, one hundred may be an over-estimate: Coast Guard records show that only six vessels were lost in the Triangle area in 1976 (twenty-eight vessels were lost off the US coast in total) and that no commercial airliner has been lost over the area in the last decade. In fact, the safety record for airliners in the Bermuda Triangle is better than over the continental United States. The evidence for a pre-ponderence of losses in the Bermuda Triangle is therefore far from crushing.

The number of small boats that go missing in the area may be due to the habits of the Florida boating population, many of whom are inexperienced and ill-equipped to cope with the problems they could meet. The sort of call which is far from uncommon was illustrated on the BBC TV documentary, *The Case For The Bermuda Triangle*, when a coast guard recalled a distress call from a woman who complained that Bimini, a very small island in the Bahamas, was not on her chart. Asked which chart she was using, the woman replied that it was the world atlas at the back of her dictionary.

Piracy may also be a contributing factor to losses in the Bermuda Triangle. Pirates or hijackers operating in the

Caribbean (the old Spanish Main, haunt of the infamous Edward Teach, better known as Blackbeard, and other fabled pirates) are thought to have claimed over six hundred yachts in the past three years, with a loss of two thousand lives!

In July 1976 the 53-foot sloop *Fiesty* was off the coast of Colombia, her four-man crew busy repairing the engine, when a rowboat silently pulled aside. Four Spanish-speaking pirates dropped to the *Fiesty*'s deck and in the ensuing struggle two of *Fiesty*'s crew were shot and killed. Their companions, Steve Johnson and David Kohler, dived over the side and were later rescued by a passing steamer.

The case of the *Fiesty* is just one of forty proven and documented cases of piracy and murder involving family pleasure craft in the Caribbean, and these forty may be only the tip of the iceberg. Congressman John Murphy, head of the Congressional subcommittee set up to investigate the growing problem of piracy, said that the actual number of vessels attacked could be much higher. 'We just don't know what happens to every boat which has disappeared in the Caribbean,' he said. 'Exactly how high the murder rate is will probably never be known. We do know that the pirates come aboard so swiftly that the yachts' crew have no time to react.' Investigations suggest that the pirates are well-financed Mafiosi and that the hijacked vessels are used to run cocaine and marijuana to the US. 'They use the vessel like a hit man uses a stolen car,' explained Marshall Philips, a Captain with the Coast Guard who has been investigating the losses. 'A couple of runs and then they scuttle it, to destroy any evidence before looking for another boat.' So the advice is: 'Know your crew well, check your voyage plan with the Coast Guard and watch out for stowaways.'

However, when all is said and done, the losses described in the books about the Bermuda Triangle are what matter. But these do not stand up to investigation. Even a cursory examination reveals gross inaccuracies: the existence of some vessels cannot be substantiated, others were unseaworthy, some disappeared during very bad weather and a few vanished in circumstances different from those most frequently described. Also, a large proportion of the losses occurred up to 150 years ago; in these cases it is impossible to know what happened.

The black-hulled *City of Glasgow* allegedly sailed into the

Bermuda Triangle in March 1854 with 480 people aboard and was never seen again. The Triangle writers rarely give more information. In fact the vessel left Liverpool on 1 March, shortly before a sister ship, *City of Manchester*, arrived in port with the news that a large ice field was crossing the route to be taken by the *City of Glasgow*. In August a certain Captain M'Leary of the bark *Mary Morris* reported that on the 18th of that month, when carefully navigating through fog-shrouded seas about six hundred miles west of Scotland, he had sighted a black-hulled vessel. A boarding party found the steamer gutted by fire and deserted. The owners of the *City of Glasgow* inclined to the view that the vessel was theirs and were naturally able to offer several possible causes of a fire, but the fate of the crew remains a mystery, although not really a very great one when you consider the chances of an over-loaded boat in stormy seas.

Three ships – the Swedish bark *Lotta*, said to have vanished north of Haiti in March 1866; the Spanish merchantman *Viego*, vanished in 1868; and the *Miramon* (or Miramonde), an Italian liner said to have disappeared en route to New Orleans in 1884 – cannot be traced. Exhaustive research has failed to identify these vessels and without corroborative evidence it is impossible to state that they vanished in the Bermuda Triangle or that they even existed.

One of the largest losses in terms of life happened in 1880 when the 923-ton *Atalanta* (not *Atlanta*, as it often appears), a British training frigate, left Bermuda with a crew of two hundred and eighty bound for Portsmouth. She never arrived. None of the Triangle writers points out that the Atlantic was subject to storms of unusual severity at the time and that a terrific storm raged along the *Atalanta*'s route from the 12th to the 16th of February. A number of ships at sea at the time are reported to have gone missing and shipping lanes were said to have been littered with debris. Moreover, all but eleven of the *Atalanta*'s crew were Royal Naval cadets who had never before been to sea in their lives.

A classic example of mis-stated evidence is in the case of the *Freya*:

On October 3, 1902, the German bark *Freya* left Manzanillo, Cuba, for Punta Arenas, Chile. On October 23 she was found listing badly, partly dismasted and abandoned by her crew. A small boarding party searched the bark and found a wall calendar in the captain's cabin bearing the date October 4, an indication that disaster overcame the vessel on or about that date. However, weather records show that only light airs prevailed at the time.

This is a summary of the story as it is most frequently told. For reasons which will shortly become apparent, the source is *Lo!*, one of four books by Charles Fort, who says that '. . . the German bark *Freya* cleared Manzanillo for Punta Arenas on the west coast of Mexico . . .'. The only problem is that there are two Manzanillos, one being a port on the west coast of Mexico and the other a port on the south-east coast of Cuba. Now it is evident that none of the Triangle writers to have told this tale bothered to check Fort's source, which he clearly gives as the 25 April 1907 issue of the journal *Nature*, where the bark is mentioned in an article about earthquakes along the *Pacific coast of Mexico*: 'Weather records show that only light winds were experienced in the region [of the *Freya*'s discovery] but, on the other hand, severe earthquakes were experienced in Acapulco and Chilpanzingo on October 4 and 5, one of which probably caused the damage to the *Freya* and led to her abandonment.' Evidently, then, the *Freya* left the Mexican Manzanillo but, whatever her port of departure, she was found in the Pacific Ocean – which is a long way away from the Atlantic's Bermuda Triangle!

Another classic twisting of facts is found in the story of the *Raifuku Maru*:

In April 1925 the Japanese freighter *Raifuku Maru* was heard calling for help, but the message she gave must be one of the weirdest in the history of maritime disasters: 'Danger like dagger now . . . come quick . . . cannot escape.' What did the radio operator mean? What kind of danger looks like a dagger? Was dagger the nearest comparison to an unearthly something that threatened and finally took the ship?

To begin with, the *Raifuku Maru* – not *Rauke Maru*, or any of the numerous other spelling variations – disappeared in 1925 – not 1921 or 1924 as is variously claimed – during a terrible storm. As for the baffling radio message, it went 'now very danger, come quick', the 'dagger' bit being pure fantasy. The SOS was picked up by the White Star liner *Homeric*, situated some seventy miles away, which sped to the freighter's aid. Mountainous seas prevented her from getting too close, however, and while *en route* she had picked up another message to the effect that all lifeboats had either been smashed or washed overboard.

The vessel SS *Cotopaxi* did disappear and her fate is unknown, but the Triangle writers usually fail to mention a radio message saying that she had water in her hold and was listing badly and that a storm, described as 'phenomenal', swept along the ship's route a few days later. Winds, which reached sixty-five miles an hour, tore along the coast of Florida, sweeping three aircraft into the sea from Daytona Beach. The *Cotopaxi*, with water in her hold and listing badly, is unlikely to have had much of a chance.

The ship *Suduffco*, said to have vanished in circumstances so mysterious that a spokesman for the owners is alleged to have said that the vessel had disappeared so completely that it was as if she had been swallowed by some gigantic sea monster, also vanished during a storm. Shortly after sailing from Port Newark, New Jersey, a Cunard liner, *Aquitania*, arrived in New York. The skipper described the sea as being the worst he had ever known.

On March 14, 1938, when the sea was 'like a millpond', the 5,456-ton steamship *Anglo-Australian*, bound from Cardiff to British Columbia, radioed that she was off Fayal in the Azores and that 'all was well'. In calm seas and under a cloudless blue sky the *Anglo-Australian* and her thirty-eight-man crew sailed into oblivion.

The exact fate of the *Anglo-Australian* is unknown, but the Triangle account of her disappearance is grossly inaccurate. On 14 March she radioed a message which, although it stated 'all well', contained the words 'rough weather'. It was later learned that gale conditions prevailed in the vicinity of the

Anglo-Australian at the time of her last message. So much for calm seas and cloudless blue skies.

On December 28, 1948, a DC-3 airliner radioed the tower at Miami airport: 'We are approaching the field . . . only fifty miles to the south . . . we can see the lights of Miami now . . . all's well. Will stand by for landing instructions.' Landing instructions were sent almost immediately, but there was no reply from the DC-3. At this time the aircraft was over an area where the water is only twenty feet deep, yet search aircraft failed to find a trace of wreckage or debris and nobody has since reported finding an old DC-3 in the region. The 'plane had vanished.

The disappearance of the DC-3 is made mysterious by the suddenness of loss of radio contact, and by an implication that the 'plane was overcome by disaster very quickly and shortly after the last radio message. This should have given search craft a clearly defined area in which they could expect to find survivors and/or wreckage. In fact this mystery-making aspect of the incident is more than adequately explained in the report of the investigation into the loss conducted by the Civil Aeronautics Board (CAB). Earlier that day the DC-3 had landed at San Juan, Puerto Rico. Her radio transmitter was not working and a repair crew found the cause to be the aircraft's batteries, which were discharged and the water level low. Advised that it would take several hours to recharge the batteries, the DC-3's captain requested that the batteries be filled with water and returned to the aircraft without charging. This was accordingly carried out. Later, during pre-takeoff procedures the San Juan tower attempted to raise the DC-3 but could not establish contact. The Chief of the Puerto Rican Transport Authority went to the aircraft and learned that the crew could receive messages but could not transmit because of weak batteries. The battery problem was not rectified and radio difficulties continued throughout the flight, several attempts to raise the aircraft proving fruitless. Thus, the DC-3 need not have been overcome by disaster shortly after her last radio message and the failure of radio contact is far from mysterious. A further point of interest concerning the final radio message is that the pilot did not say that he could see the lights of Miami nor was he in communication with Miami tower at that time. The radio message was intercepted by the radio station at New Orleans and nowhere in the CAB report or in newspaper reports is there any mention of the pilot seeing the lights of Miami. It would seem that the Triangle writers assumed that the DC-3 was fifty miles from Miami because the pilot said so and assumed that he would therefore be able to see the lights. In fact the DC-3's position was only an estimate and could have been in error by up to a hundred miles.

The DC-3's precise position *is* uncertain. The pilot had been told to expect a wind from the northwest as he approached Miami, but the wind had shifted during the flight and, although news of the wind shift had been radioed to the aircraft it is uncertain whether it was received. If not, the 'plane could have drifted off course, going so far south that she would have missed the southern tip of Florida and flown on into the Gulf of Mexico. She had only an hour's worth of fuel left in the tanks and, deprived of her radio, this would have produced a critical situation. As for the claim that the aircraft was over shallow water when she disappeared, there is no way of knowing this for certain: the DC-3 could have vanished over the Gulf, as stated; however, only a small portion of the ocean in the vicinity of the DC-3's assumed position when she vanished is in fact shallow, elsewhere the ocean reaches depths of up to five thousand feet. Moreover, this is the place where the turbulent Gulf Stream flows.

> In June 1950 the 350-foot Costa Rican freighter *Sandra* and her crew of twenty eight sailed from Savannah, Georgia, through the tropic dusk and peaceful weather to Puerto Cabello, Venezuela. Hugging the Florida coastline and able to see the glow of the lights from various waterfront cities – where there were rescue 'planes less than one hour's flying time distant – the *Sandra* slipped through placid seas and vanished.

The Costa Rican freighter SS *Sandra* did vanish *en route* from Savannah to Venezuela, but that's about the sum total of accuracy in the popular Bermuda Triangle version of the tale. The *Sandra* was 185 feet and not 350 feet long; she carried a crew of eleven and not twenty eight; she sailed in April and not June 1950; and the seas were stormy and battered by hurricane-force winds rather than being placid, calm and tranquil.

One New Year's Eve (1957–58) Harvey Conover and four companions left Key West, Florida, bound for Miami aboard Conover's forty-four-foot yacht *Revonoc*. It was a voyage of only one hundred and fifty miles and the yacht would never be out of sight of land, but it was nevertheless a one hundred and fifty mile voyage through the deadly Bermuda Triangle . . .

. . . and wind-lashed seas and near-hurricane winds in the worst midwinter storm in the history of southern Florida.

One of the supposedly baffling mysteries of the Bermuda Triangle involves two KC-135 stratotankers which vanished some 335 miles southwest of Bermuda in August 1963. A mass of debris was subsequently found near the aircraft's last reported position and it was assumed that the tankers had collided in mid-air. However, some time later a second concentration of wreckage from a KC-135 was found 160 miles from the original crash site, invalidating the theory of a mid-air collision and raising the question: how and why did the KC-135s crash 160 miles apart?

The answer to this impossibility is that they didn't. Contrary to the Triangle legend, the second concentration of wreckage was *not* proved conclusively to have been from one of the KC-135s. The *Miami Herald* of 1 September quotes Major Fred Brent of the Air Rescue Service at Orlando Air Force Base as saying: 'It appears to be just a large patch of seaweed, driftwood and an old buoy.' It was sighted on 30 August, as the sun was about to set, when visibility was far from good, and reported in the press the following morning before search craft had reached the location.

On March 21, 1973, M/S *Anita*, laden with a cargo of coal and carrying a crew numbering thirty-two, sailed from Newport News for Germany. Like so many ships before her, she entered the Bermuda Triangle and – vanished. A characteristically thorough search established that the

20,000-ton vessel had completely disappeared. Lloyd's of London paid 3,000,000 dollars to the ship's owners. A short time later the *Anita*'s sister ship, the *Norse Varient*, also disappeared.

The M/S *Anita* was a 13,000-ton freighter, not 20,000-ton. She left Newport News two hours after the *Norse Varient*. Both ships were carrying the same cargo and bound for the same destination. Two days after leaving port the *Norse Varient* ran into a severe storm. The sea was running thirty-five to forty-five feet high and winds were reaching eighty-five miles an hour. Just after noon a radio message was received from the vessel stating that she was foundering 150 miles southeast of Cape May, New Jersey.

One man lived to tell of what had happened aboard *Norse Varient*. He was picked up after three days afloat on a large orange raft. He said that a forty-by-forty-foot hatch cover had been ripped off during the storm and that towering seas had quickly flooded two cargo holds. The *Norse Varient* sank within five minutes after the order had been given to abandon ship.

The M/S *Anita*, following the same route as the *Norse Varient* and travelling only a matter of hours behind her sister ship, no doubt encountered the same storm and suffered the same or a similar fate. In the *Anita*'s case, however, no SOS was sent and there were no survivors. Debris was found in the shape of a life ring bearing the vessel's name. It does not seem unlikely that savage seas caused the loss of the *Anita*, not some death ray from Atlantis, a UFO or some magnetic anomaly.

Such examples as these could go on and on, but it is already evident that the 'Bermuda Triangle mystery' is founded on evidence that is grossly inaccurate. As for the theories, these too do not bear close inspection. For example, the precise location of the Devil's Sea is rather vague, which is a bit awkward if you want to avoid it. The Bermuda Triangle writers are far from precise:

CHARLES BERLITZ and VINCENT GADDIS	South or southeast of Japan, between Japan and the Bonin Islands.

JOHN GODWIN	Between Iwo Jima and Marcus Island.
ADI-KENT THOMAS JEFFREY and JOHN WALLACE SPENCER	Between Japan and the Marianas Islands.
ELIZABETH NICHOLS	A triangle connecting Japan, Wake Island and Guam.
IVAN T. SANDERSON	250 miles south of Honshu, about longitude 140 degrees.
RICHARD WINER	A triangle bounded by the southeast coast of Japan, the northeast tip of the Phillippines, and Guam.

A glance at the map on page 84 will illustrate just how these locations differ.

Most accounts of the Devil's Sea mention that it is an official danger zone, that in 1955 a survey ship trying to find the cause of the losses in the area itself vanished, and that a score of ships and aircraft have disappeared there. Few of the accounts give any details of the dozens of vessels to have vanished in the Devil's Sea – and Lawrence David Kusche, a research librarian at the Arizona State University who investigated the Triangle for his book *The Bermuda Triangle Mystery – Solved*, had considerable difficulty in finding somebody in Japan who had ever heard of the place. However, the facts about the Devil's Sea are as follows:

It is claimed that between 1950 and 1954 no less than nine large coastal freighters mysteriously vanished in the Devil's Sea. Names are rarely given, but research suggests that the vessels referred to are *No. 1 Guro Sio Maru, No. 2 Guro Sio Maru, Chyo Huku Maru, Kaiyo Maru, Shin Shei Maru, No. 3 Guro Sio Maru, Fa Yu Maru, Shei Shyo Maru,* and *Ko Zi Maru.* They were not all large coastal freighters, but small fishing vessels ranging from 62 to 190 tons, and they did not all have radios. Moreover, they vanished between April 1949 and October 1953. Of particular interest is the fourth vessel to have disappeared, *Kaiyo Maru*; this is the research vessel supposedly sent out in 1955. In fact, the vessel disappeared in 1952 (which, to be fair, is the date given by two Triangle writers, Vincent Gaddis and John Wallace Spencer) while

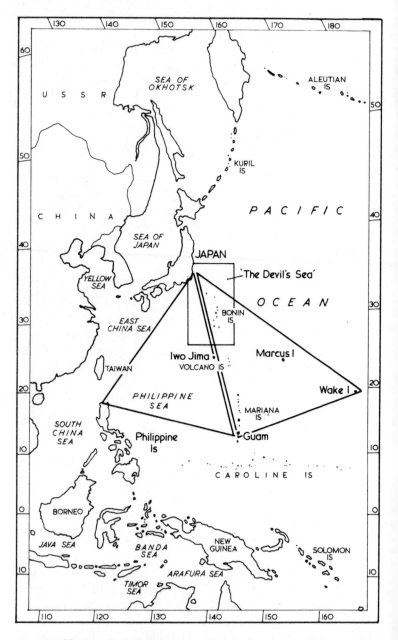

The Devil's Sea is usually said to lie off the coast of Japan – but
where? Nobody seems to agree and, as the map shows, the views can
be conflicting. The actual 'Devil's Sea' is also shown.

observing the birth of a new island thrust up to the surface by a volcanic eruption. The volcano erupted for a second time while the ship was in the vicinity and it is almost certain that the *Kaiyo Maru* was destroyed either by the eruption or by the resultant tidal wave.

The most interesting result from this information is that by plotting the approximate location of each loss we can establish the precise area of the Devil's Sea: it is an oblong area some 750 miles long! So much for a relatively small area off the coast of Japan!

As for the remaining Vile Vortices discovered by Ivan T. Sanderson, I suspect that his research leaves much to be desired. Any well travelled region will show a higher percentage of losses than a poorly travelled one, so a large number of losses in one region is not evidence of an anomaly. Moreover, each disappearance demands close examination – was the ship seaworthy?, what were the aquatic and atmospheric conditions prevailing at the time?, does the nature of the accident preclude natural causes?, was the crew competent?, and so on. Sanderson's 'discovery' was not based on statistical evidence of this kind at all.

The compass needle does not point to the actual North Pole but rather to the magnetic North Pole and navigators must take account of the distance between the poles when plotting a course. However, in certain parts of the world the actual and magnetic Poles lie in a straight line – the Agonic Line – and one such place is off the coast of Florida.

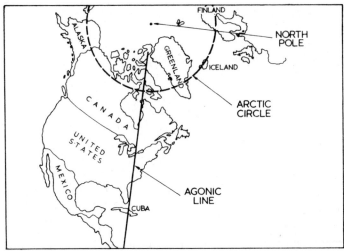

Moving on to the theories, the most absurd suggestion is that the disappearances are caused by a magnetic anomaly connected in some way with the fact that in the Bermuda Triangle the compass needle points to the actual North Pole rather than the magnetic North Pole. The magnetic North Pole is situated on the Boothia Peninsula, the most northerly point on the North American mainland, and it was discovered on 31 May 1831 by the explorer Sir James Clark Ross. As the map on page 85 illustrates, at certain places in the world the actual North Pole and the magnetic North Pole are bound to be in a straight line, the Agonic Line; along which a compass will point to both actual and magnetic North. The Agonic Line runs just off the coast of Florida, and as you move away from it so the distance between the direction to the magnetic and the actual North Pole increases. This increase and corresponding decrease is known as magnetic variation or magnetic declination; navigators account for it as a routine part of navigation. Not to take account of it could lead a ship or 'plane off course – but not off the coast of Florida: here you are safer than elsewhere.

As for Wilbert B. Smith's discovery of 'areas of reduced binding', his Project Magnet was neither conducted on behalf of nor sponsored by the Department of Transport or the Canadian Government and his conclusions do not represent official views. Smith's discovery was made with an instrument of his own invention and has not been duplicated. Moreover, his discovery was not made public in an official report but through the Spring 1963 issue of the *Journal* of the Ottowa UFO Club.

The United States Navy's Project Magnet is somewhat different. This was a geomagnetic survey of the world: places with high iron-ore deposits, for example, have their own magnetic fields and near them compasses cannot be trusted; these places are therefore well worth surveying. Project Magnet was an attempt to map such places, the magnetic maps then in use being long out of date.

Project Magnet developed an aura of mystery in 1963 when its existence was 'revealed' in an article, 'US Special Project Linked To UFOs', in the June-September issue of *UFO Investigator*. A reporter for that journal explained how he had 'discovered' a military aircraft on an auxiliary runway at San

Francisco Airport. He struck up a conversation with the 'plane's non-uniformed crew and learned that they were engaged on a 'carefully unpublicized program'. The 'plane was involved in a secret Navy project called Magnet – the reporter learned this because the Navy had cunningly concealed their activities by painting PROJECT MAGNET in huge block letters on the tail of the 'plane. The non-uniformed crew revealed that strange magnetic forces had been discovered in an area of the Caribbean where five Navy aircraft had vanished in 1945 (obviously Flight-19) and that they were due to investigate the region in an effort to find the source of the anomalies. However, the reporter deduced that the real mission was to do with UFOs!

The Bermuda Triangle mystery is based on the belief that a large number of ships and aircraft have vanished and are continuing to vanish without reason and that they are connected and/or caused by a force for which science has no explanation. To support this view large numbers of examples are cited.

In reality the examples are littered with erroneous material, more prosaic explanations seem to have been deliberately avoided and in some cases the accounts contain data which is contrary to the truth. The quality of research is generally very poor, facts have been manipulated and information twisted and distorted to give the wrong impression. When the true facts are presented the foundation of the Bermuda Triangle mystery crumbles and the case for the Bermuda Triangle collapses into dust. If anybody wishes to claim otherwise they must present evidence which is good evidence. The burden of proof is on those who make such claims, not upon the sceptics. In short, the Bermuda Triangle is a myth, or, as Lawrence Kusche put it, 'probably one of the best hoaxes that has ever been pulled off'.

8 *Mary Celeste*

In December 1872 the American brigantine *Mary Celeste* was found aimlessly drifting in the Atlantic. She was boarded and found to be in good condition, seaworthy and well provisioned; but her crew had disappeared. How the *Mary Celeste* came to be in this condition and what fate befell her crew is one of the great mysteries of the sea.

Almost everybody has heard of the *Mary Celeste*, but precisely what they have heard, fantasy or fact, is another matter. Over the past hundred years a cocoon of myth has grown around the story, embellishing and gradually superseding the facts, and it is not uncommon to find fables (such as a freshly prepared meal being found in the galley) presented as fact in outwardly intelligent and authoritative accounts. Fortunately, there is a considerable amount of dependable contemporary information and several reliable accounts from which it is possible to derive an accurate history.

Although the principal element of the ship's story is the disappearance of her crew in 1872, that is really but one incident in a twenty-eight year history of misfortune. The *Mary Celeste* was a jinxed ship, a hoodoo vessel cursed by misfortune from the day she was launched until the day she was deliberately run aground and set on fire.

The early history of *Mary Celeste* (not *Marie Celeste*) is confused, and reliable information difficult to find, but we do know that she began life under the name *Amazon*. She was built at Spencer's Island, Nova Scotia, in 1860, the maiden venture of a consortium of pioneer shipbuilders, and, according to the records, launched in the spring of 1861 from the shipyards of Joshua Dewis.

Amazon was a brigantine (a twin-masted vessel, square rigged on the foremast and fore-and-aft rigged on the mainmast), wooden-shelled, carvel-built,* and constructed of maple, birch and beech up to the light load line, spruce to the rails and pine to finish the cabins. She was small, only 99.3 feet long, 25.5 feet across the beam and 11.7 feet deep. Her gross weight was 198.42 tons.

Tragedy struck *Amazon* not many weeks after the launch when her skipper, a proud young Scot named Robert McLellan, fell sick and died. Her new captain, John Nutting Parker, took *Amazon* on her maiden voyage: she ran into a fishing weir off Maine, receiving a large gash in her hull, and was sent to the shipyards for repairs. While she was there a fire broke out amidships and Captain Parker lost his job.

Amazon's third skipper took her across the Atlantic: she collided with a brig when entering the Straits of Dover. The brig went to the bottom, *Amazon* went to the shipyards for repairs and the skipper went to look for another job.

The ownership history is now shrouded in uncertainty. It is said that, following the necessary repairs and the appointment of a new skipper, *Amazon* returned across the Atlantic and ran aground off Cow Bay, Cape Breton Island, in northeast Nova Scotia. Some accounts say that she was pulled off the rocks by a certain Alexander McBean or was pulled off and sold to McBean; and he is alleged to have spent 16,000 dollars on repairs, changing the name from *Amazon* to *Mary Celeste* in the process. However, McBean apparently went bankrupt, and the vessel was seized and auctioned in New York, being bought by a certain John Beatty. Beatty seems to have been no more fortunate than McBean, for he too went bankrupt and the ship was auctioned yet again.

Another account maintains that *Amazon* was sold in public auction and that her new owners changed her name to *Mary Celeste,* registering the change on 31 December 1868. She subsequently changed hands several times before being bought by J. H. Winchester and Co., a consortium of New York shipowners.

---

*Carvel-built vessels were those in which the side planks are all flush, the edges laid close together and the seams filled with oakum (tarred hemp or manila fibres made from old ropes which have been unpicked), over which hot pitch was poured to prevent the oakum from rotting and to make the vessel watertight. The alternative to carvel construction is clinker or clinch building, in which the planks overlap.

A third account maintains that the vessel was bought by J. H. Winchester in 1869.

In any event, by 1872 *Amazon* was owned by a consortium, the principal shareholder being James H. Winchester, who held twelve twenty-fourths or one half. The other shareholders were Benjamin Spooner Briggs with eight twenty-fourths and Sylvester Goodwin and Daniel T. Sampson with two twenty-fourths apiece. A mortgage on the vessel was held by a certain Mr Hart.

By this time the *Amazon* was unrecognisable. She was now a hermaphrodite brig,* she had an extended deck cabin and a new copper bottom and her dimensions had been increased to 103 feet in length, 25.7 feet across the beam; her weight was 282.28 tons. She was registered as an American vessel, flew the American flag and her name was *Mary Celeste*. We don't know if the name had any special significance, but it is certainly odd, 'Mary' being English and 'Celeste' being French. One suggestion is that the name was the result of a painter's error, the name being intended to be *Mary Sellers* or even, perhaps, *Marie Celeste*.

Special attention should here be given to the captain and crew. Many theories over the past century picture the crew as a disreputable and unruly bunch of cut-throats and pirates next to whom Blackbeard looks like a saint. One notable book, *The Great Mary Celeste Hoax*, replaces the known crew with an imaginary and motley collection of brawling bullies of whom any dastardly deed would have been in character, yet the truth is that *Mary Celeste*'s crew were all of good character and considerably better than the average windjammer crew.

The captain was Benjamin Spooner Briggs: born at Wareham, Massachusetts, on 24 April 1835, he was the second of five sons born to Captain Nathan Briggs and his wife Sophia (née Cobb). It was a seafaring family: four of the brothers went to sea and two of the four became master mariners at an early age. At the age of 38, when he took

---

*A hermaphrodite brig, sometimes known as a brig-schooner, was rigged on the foremast as a brig, with square sails set on the yards, and on the mainmast as a schooner, with a square topsail set above a gaff mainsail. She differed from a brigantine by the square topsail set on the mainmast, brigantines being fully fore-and-aft rigged on the mainmast.

command of *Mary Celeste*, Benjamin had already commanded three vessels: the schooner *Forest King*, the bark *Arthur*, and the brigantine *Sea Foam*. He was a stern-faced New England Puritan and deeply religious. He regularly read his Bible and observed a strict abstinence from alcohol, following his father's rule of never allowing the 'demon drink' on board his ship. Following Benjamin's disappearance, Horatio Sprague, the United States Consul in Gibraltar, where Briggs was a member of St John's Lodge of Masons, wrote to N. W. Bingham, a Treasury Department Agent in Boston, saying that Captain Briggs 'always bore the highest character as a Christian and as an intelligent and active shipmaster'. Again, in a letter dated 20 January 1873, to the Department of State, Consul Sprague wrote, 'he was well known' and 'bore the highest character for seamanship and correctness'.

Benjamin Spooner Briggs, then, was a man who held clearly defined moral views and rightfully expected those who sailed under his command to abide by them. He was stern and not the sort of man to be imposed upon or abused, but he was a good man, liked and respected, and no doubt just and considerate to his crew.

Benjamin was accompanied on the voyage by his wife and daughter. His wife was a distant cousin, the daughter of the parson of the Congregational Church in Marion, Massachusetts. She and Benjamin had been childhood sweethearts and had married in 1862, when he was twenty-seven and she twenty. They had two children; the eldest, a son, Arthur Stanley, was seven and had recently begun his schooling. The youngest was two-year-old Sophia Matilda.

In the National Archives, Washington, D.C., there is a list of the crew. The First Mate was Albert G. Richardson. He had served as a private in the American Civil War. His wife, Frances, was a niece of James H. Winchester. He had sailed under Captain Briggs before and was trustworthy, competent and held in high regard.

Little is known about the Second Mate, Andrew Gilling, beyond what is given in the official record. His birthplace is given as New York, but there is reason to believe that he was of Danish extraction. A letter dated 8 July 1873 from the pastor of the parish of Kathy Samso, Denmark, to the Danish consul in Gibraltar, inquires on behalf of Gilling's mother, described as being 'bereaved and sorrowful', regarding her son's fate and the proper procedure for acquiring her son's personal effects.

The cook and steward was Edward William Head. In an article in the New York *Sunday World* on 24 January 1886 an article quotes Captain Winchester as saying that Head 'belonged to Williamsburg, Brooklyn, New York, where he was respected by all who knew him'. He had married not long before sailing on *Mary Celeste* and there is on record a letter from his wife, Emma, asking for her husband's effects.

The remainder of the crew was composed of four seamen of German birth and very little is known about them. Two were brothers, Volkert and Boy or Boz Lorenzen, who hailed from the Island of Fohr in the North Sea. A third, Arian Martens, came from Suddorf on the neighbouring island of Amrum. All three were known to T. A. Nickelsen, Chief of the Parish of Utersum, who wrote letters to the German Consul and the United States Consul at Gibraltar inquiring on behalf of the grieving mother of the Lorenzens about her sons and asking for their effects. Both the Lorenzens and Arian Martens were respected in their communities. Volkert Lorenzen and Martens were married with children and Boy or Boz Lorenzen was engaged. Ironically, the letter explained that the Lorenzen brothers had lost all their possessions in a shipwreck prior to signing aboard *Mary Celeste*.

Of the last crew member there is very little known indeed. His name is variously spelt – Gottliechs Goodschadd, Gottlied Gottschalk, and others. It is probable that he hailed from the Island of Fohr where the name 'Gottschalk' is known.

That the men were all of good character is evidenced by the number of letters from friends and family, and we know that Captain Briggs was reasonably happy with them. In a letter dated 7 November 1872 Sarah Briggs wrote to Benjamin's mother: 'Benj thinks we have got a pretty peaceable lot this time all round, if they continue as they have begun.'

Sometime during late September or early October 1872 *Mary Celeste* arrived in New York with a cargo of coal from Cow Bay, Nova Scotia. She berthed at Pier 44, in New York's East River, about a mile from James H. Winchester's office, and the coal was unloaded. There was a change of crew and Mate Richardson took temporary command to supervise the

loading of the new cargo, 1,701 barrels of commercial alcohol*
being shipped by Meissner Ackerman and Co., merchants of
New York, to H. Mascerenhas and Co., of Genoa, Italy, for
use in fortifying wine. After about three weeks Captain Briggs
took command. The loading was completed late on Saturday
2 November and, early on 5 November, *Mary Celeste* was
towed from Pier 44 by the Sandy Hook pilot ship to the lower
bay off Staten Island. According to the Disaster Books of the
Atlantic Mutual Insurance Company, one of *Mary Celeste's*
insurers, the Atlantic was unusually stormy for the time of
year and the New York *Maritime Register*, quoting from the
logs of steamers from Europe, gives a bleak picture of an
ocean swept by violent seas and tremendous gales. As a result
of fierce headwinds *Mary Celeste* dropped anchor off Staten
Island for two days before venturing out to sea on Thursday
7 November. *Mary Celeste* would make many more voyages,
but for those aboard it was to be their last.

On 15 November 1872, eight days after *Mary Celeste* left
New York, the 295 ton brigantine *Dei Gratia*, under the command of a bewhiskered Nova Scotian named David Reed
Morehouse, left the Venango Yard, Hoboken, New York,
bound for Gibraltar and then Genoa with a cargo of petroleum.
The voyage proceeded without any unusual incidents until
4 December. At noon the afternoon watch, consisting of
Second Mate John Wright and two seamen, Augustus Anderson
and John Johnson, came on duty. Shortly after one o'clock
Captain Morehouse came on deck. Wright pointed to a sail
about five or six miles distant on the weather bow (port). The
vessel was heading in a westerly direction, the opposite
direction from *Dei Gratia*, which was SE by E. The wind was
from the north, yet the vessel was on a starboard tack.
Evidently there was something wrong. Morehouse surveyed the
vessel through his glass and judged from the lack of sails that
she was indeed in trouble. He summoned his First Mate, a
burly Canadian named Oliver Deveau, from below deck and

---

*The value of *Mary Celeste's* cargo has been variously given, and one
well known author on the subject has even claimed that the cargo was not
insured. In fact the cargo was insured abroad – as far as I can establish, in
Hamburg – by its shippers, Meissner Ackerman and Co., a 'very respectable'
company of New York, for $36,943. Further to this, J. H. Winchester and
Co. insured the freight on charter – i.e., the amount of money the company
expected to receive upon delivery of the cargo – with the Atlantic Mutual
Insurance Company for $3,400.

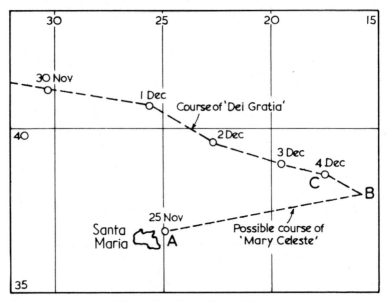

The route of the *Mary Celeste*.

handed him the glass. Deveau scanned the vessel with a practised eye and concurred with his opinion. The two men decided to haul wind and hail her.

At three o'clock Morehouse hailed the stranger. There was no reply and it was decided to lower the boat. Deveau, with Second Mate John Wright and seaman Johnson, rowed across to the stranger. Johnson pulled the boat alongside and Deveau and Wright hauled themselves over the stranger's railings and dropped to the deck. They were greeted by an eerie silence.

The first thing Deveau did was sound the pumps, thinking that the vessel might have sustained underwater damage. The ship's pump was forward of the main mast; nearby the sounding rod was lying on the deck, evidence that somebody had sounded the vessel not long before whatever fate befell her crew, as otherwise the rod would have been returned to its proper place. Deveau dropped the sounding rod down the pump well and to his amazement found only three and a half feet of water in the hold. This showed that the vessel was leaking only a small amount.

Deveau and Wright spent about an hour aboard the vessel, which they learned to be *Mary Celeste*. They searched her from stem to stern. The main staysail, which was thought to be missing, was found on the foreward house, but the foresail and upper foresail were missing, having been blown from the yards and lost. The jib, fore-topmast staysail and the fore lower topsail were set, the last hanging by four corners. The remaining sails were furled. Some of the running rigging was fouled, some had been blown away, and parts were hanging over the sides. The main peak halyard (the ropes used to hoist the outer end of the gaff sail) was 'broke and gone', as Deveau put it. All were indications that the vessel had encountered heavy weather.

The wheel was free, another sign that the crew must have left the ship in a hurry; it was the act of but a moment (and instinct) to lash the wheel. The binnacle was knocked down and broken.

The main hatch was well battened and secure, but the fore and lazaretto hatch covers had been removed and were found lying near the hatchways, although there does not seem to be any evidence for the often repeated frequent claim that the hatch covers were lying the wrong side up, a sign of misfortune to superstitious seamen.

There was less than a foot of water in the galley; a nine-inch doorsill had prevented the water from running out. The stove had been knocked out of place, but the kitchen utensils were all clean and in their proper places in the pantry. About six months' worth of supplies and provisions were in the lazarreto and there was plenty of fresh water.

The crew's personal possessions were in the forecastle. They had left clothing, boots, oil-skins and, significantly, their pipes and tobacco, items which no sailor would leave behind unless in fear for his life.

Water had entered the captain's cabin through a skylight, which was open and bore a large hole in one pane of glass. Bedding and clothing were soaked and there were puddles on the floor. The bed, which was unmade, bore the impression of a child's body. The ship's strongbox was found safely locked. There were a few pieces of Mrs Briggs' jewellery on a small table; an expensive clock, ruined by water; and under the captain's bed Deveau found a valuable Italian sword, apparently stained with blood. On the table lay the log slate (temporary log), which read: 'Monday, 25th. At five o'clock made island of St Mary's [Santa Maria in the Azores] bearing

ESE. At eight o'clock Eastern point bore SSW six miles distant.'

In the Mate's cabin Deveau found a chart showing the track of *Mary Celeste* up to 24 November. It showed that the vessel had gone south of the Azores, turning north after passing Santa Maria.

Deveau did not find the Celeste's chronometer, sextant, bill of lading, navigation book, or other of the ship's papers. Also missing was the ship's boat, a yawl about sixteen to twenty feet long with nine to twelve inches of freeboard. It had been carried lashed to the main hatch, but this spot was now empty and a piece of railing running alongside had been removed, apparently to launch the craft. Obviously Captain Briggs and his crew had abandoned ship and done so in a hurry, but why? The vessel was in good condition and Augustus Anderson, one of *Dei Gratia*'s crew, later said that she was in a fit state to go around the world. What, then, could have prompted Captain Briggs to put his family and crew into a heavily overloaded yawl and desert a seaworthy ship for the stormy Atlantic?

Deveau, Wright and Johnson returned to *Dei Gratia* and reported to Captain Morehouse. Deveau was keen to take *Mary Celeste* into Gibraltar and claim her as salvage. Under international maritime law the salvager of an abandoned vessel acquires a lien upon that vessel: a percentage of the *Mary Celeste* and her cargo might have netted the *Dei Gratia*'s crew up to $80,000. Captain Morehouse was not interested in the money, however, but in the safety of his men and ship. He eventually consented, however, and gave Deveau two men, Augustus Anderson and Charles Lund, a barometer, compass and watch. Deveau took his own nautical instruments and whatever food the steward had prepared.

It took him about two days to restore *Mary Celeste* to order before the two ships could proceed with the voyage. Fortunately they had good weather. Six hundred miles lay between them and Gibraltar and, with only three men to man each ship, a storm would most likely have proved fatal. However, on the night of Wednesday 11 December, having passed Cape Spartel, Morocco, and entered the Straits of Gibraltar, they ran into a rain storm and became separated. *Mary Celeste* was forced to anchor under the Ceuta light, some thirty-five

1 To vanish successfully is far from easy: there are too many ways of being caught out, as the boy in the foreground of this photograph discovered. On the Missing Persons list, he just happened to be around when a press photographer snapped actor Roger Moore walking through Berwick Market in London. Relatives recognized him when the photograph appeared in the London *Daily Express*, and the search for him intensified. *(London Express News and Feature Services.)*

HUNT FOR GIRL SHIFTED

Bennington Official Believes Student Met With Foul Play

Special to THE NEW YORK TIMES.

BENNINGTON, Vt., Dec. 5— Search in the wooded area of this countryside for Miss Paula Welden of Stamford, Conn., 18-year-old Bennington College student, was abandoned tonight after State's Attorney William T. Jerome Jr. advanced a theory of possible foul play.

He ordered broadcast a description of a half-ton truck, bearing New York registration plates, which was seen on Long Trail over Glastonbury Mountain at the same time as Miss Welden last Sunday night.

Seven Marine Corps planes from the Squantum, Mass., Naval Air Station flew over this area today, but were forced to give up because of low-hanging clouds.

2 NEW DETECTIVES JOIN WELDEN HUNT

But Little Is Turned Up in the Search for Girl Missing at Bennington College

Special to THE NEW YORK TIMES.

BENNINGTON, Vt., Dec. 12— As two Connecticut detectives delved into the mysterious disappearance of 18-year-old Paula Welden from Bennington College, Gov. Mortimer R. Proctor twice telephoned the State's Attorney here today asking that he be kept fully informed of all developments.

There was little of a hopeful nature, however, in today's developments. If any clues have been turned up they have not been made public by the authorities.

The girl, daughter of W. Archibald Welden of Stamford, Conn., dropped from sight on Dec. 1 when she left her dormitory room late in the afternoon to take a walk. Townsfolk, college students and volunteers from other sections have toiled up and down Glastonbury Mountain, where she was reported seen, in a fruitless search. Searching parties continued their cold and weary task today.

The girl's father, who has made two trips to undisclosed points in the search, has reiterated that he believes his daughter was abducted. Several men have been questioned by Vermont authorities.

The two Connecticut investigators were called into the case at the request of Mr. Welden. He asked Governor Proctor to seek aid from Gov. Raymond E. Baldwin of Connecticut, who responded by sending Lieuts. Robert N. Rundle and Dora C. Scoville. The two were absent during the morning on an undisclosed mission. Upon their return they asked all officials who were on Glastonbury or Bald Mountains the day Miss Welden disappeared to get in touch with them.

Mrs. Scoville questioned Elizabeth Johnson, the missing girl's roommate, for several hours.

Mr. Welden turned over to State's Attorney William T. Jerome Jr. four anonymous notes he had received. He did not disclose their contents.

Investigators have been sent to New Hampshire, Massachusetts and New York on "tips."

All that appears to be known is that the girl waited on table at noon wearing a green smock. After she had finished and had her own dinner she changed into blue dungarees, donned a red parka and set out for a walk.

2 (above) & 3 (below) Paula Welden was perhaps the most celebrated victim of the "Mad murderer of the Long Trail" in Vermont. Late in 1946 she went out for a walk and, despite a colossal search, as reported in these contemporary news reports from The New York Times, she was never seen again: indeed, no trace of her was ever found. (Author's Collection.)

WELDEN ENDS HIS SEARCH

Father of Missing Girl Leaves Bennington to Return Home

BENNINGTON, Vt., Dec. 15 (AP) —W. Archibald Welden, whose 18-year-old daughter, Paula, disappeared without trace from the Bennington College campus two weeks ago, left here for his Stamford (Conn.) home today. He said he would not return "unless something important comes up."

Mr. Welden took his daughter's belongings back to Stamford with him.

William Travers Jerome Jr., State's Attorney, after an investigation that spread into New York and Connecticut, said that "all clues have been run down and found unavailing."

Dressed in a red parka, blue jeans and sneakers, Paula disappeared Dec. 1 after telling friends she was going on a hike. Intensive search of Glastonbury Mountain, where she was reported seen, has uncovered no clues.

Jesse Watson, Bennington game warden, nevertheless arranged to search the long trail area again tomorrow. With him will be five other woodsmen and Watson's hound dog.

TO DIG FOR MISSING GIRL

Search for Vermont Co-Ed Leads to Gravel Pit

Special to The New York Times.

BENNINGTON, Vt., Dec. 16—A gravel pit near the entrance to Bennington College will be excavated tomorrow in the search for Paula Welden, 18-year-old sophomore who disappeared on Dec. 1, State's Attorney William T. Jerome, Jr. announced tonight.

The decision to dig into the pit came after five woodsmen with a hunting dog returned without a clue after an all-day search along the long trail on Glastoy Mountain.

Authorities said that residents in the vicinity of the gravel pit had reported seeing a landslide there Dec. 1. Lt. Robert N. Rundle of the Connecticut State Police, said it was possible that Miss Welden had attempted to climb the 75-foot bank at the pit and caused the slide.

Mr. Jerome said that an attendant at the gasoline station had reported seeing a girl running up a knoll near the pit.

No plans were made for a further search in the wooded area which has been combed in the last two weeks by college students, townspeople and volunteers from this section.

WELDEN MAKES YULE PLEA

'Come Home, We Love You,' Says Missing Girl's Father on Air

STAMFORD, Conn., Dec. 23 (UP) In a poignant Christmas appeal, the father of Paula Welden begged the missing Bennington College student tonight to come home "to your mother and sisters who love you so much."

W. Archibald Welden, industrial engineer, broadcast his appeal on a Stamford radio station as authorities in Bennington, Vt., officially abandoned search for the girl who disappeared from the college campus Dec. 1.

"Paula, in just two more days it will be Christmas," the father said in his plea. "If this appeal reaches you, know that we love you and want you.

"Whatever prompted you to leave us, if you have gone of your own free will, be sure that we can find a better answer to your problem by working on it together.

"Wherever you are, just pick up the nearest telephone and ask for me. You won't need money. Just ask the operator to reverse the charges.

"I will come for you immediately, wherever you are, and bring you back home to your mother and sisters who love you so much and miss you so terribly."

Hitch-hike killer hunt

DEAD: Hitch-hiker Heidi Reddin.

BOYS STUMBLE INTO HORROR

By PETER KANE

THE MURDER of schoolgirl Heidi Reddin may be only the latest in a series of brutal killings.

Police last night re-opened the files on the unsolved murders of two other girls in a bid to find a link.

And they were also checking records of three disappearances which have baffled them for years.

The search began as another hunt ended—in tragedy.

Six weeks after 14-year-old Heidi vanished two boys found her half-naked body in a water-

filled ditch just two miles from her home at Downham Market in Norfolk.

She disappeared on December 15 while thumbing a lift on the nearby A10 road

Detective Superintendent Bill Curry, deputy head of Norfolk C.I.D., said last night: "Obviously, there is a killer around.

" And when one thinks of this inquiry one thinks of previous occurrences like it."

Meanwhile, his men were examining the files on:

● Susan Long, 18, found strangled and sexually assaulted near her home at Norwich in 1970.

● The discovery of the

DEAD: Susan Long

MISSING: April Fabb

headless body of a woman in woods at Swaffham, Norfolk, in 1974.

● April Fabb and Steven Newing—both 13—who vanished from their homes in Norfolk in 1969, and were never found.

● Pam Exall, 21, who disappeared in 1974 while on holiday at

MISSING: Steven Newing

Shettisham in Norfolk.

Supt. Curry said, "All these mysteries have occupied the minds of every policeman for some considerable time.

"We are looking at their files again."

He said of Heidi: "She could have been mistaken for being a lot older than she really was."

MISSING: Pam Exall

4 Faces of the missing: one of the reports of the search for the East Anglian hitch-hike killer.

(*Daily Mirror.*)

5 Charles Berlitz, although not the first to write about the Bermuda Triangle, has written two books which, extraordinarily successful on an international scale, have brought the region to the attention of the world. More recent workers have questioned his research methods and shown many of his evidence to be at best dubious, but nevertheless in the minds of the public he has proved his case. *(Souvenir Press.)*

6 Five TBF bombers of the type of which the notorious Flight 19 was composed. *(US Navy Photograph.)*

7 A PBY, known as a "flying gas tank" because of the quantity of fuel it carried, of the type which set out to search for Flight 19 – to disappear in its turn. *(US Navy Photograph.)*

8 The *Star Tiger*, which vanished *en route* to Bermuda. To this day, and despite an extensive official inquiry, nobody knows what caused the loss. (*Press Association.*)

EXPRESS & ECHO

£1,000 REWARD

for information leading directly to the safe return of

GENETTE TATE

Contact the nearest policeman or ring
Woodbury 35111 or 35112 or Exeter 73051

9 Genette Tate, out on her bicycle delivering newspapers in Devon in late summer 1978, vanished completely only a few minutes after speaking with friends: a nationwide poster campaign, a vigorous police hunt, and sustained effort on the part of countless individuals failed to produce any clues whatsoever as to her whereabouts. *(Exeter Express and Echo.)*

miles eastward along the Moroccan coast, and wait for daylight. Meanwhile, *Dei Gratia* arrived in Gibraltar in the evening of 12 December. *Mary Celeste* arrived the following day.

Within two hours of dropping anchor *Mary Celeste* was placed under arrest by Thomas J. Vecchio, Marshal of the Vice Admiralty Court. Captain Morehouse and his crew were certainly entitled to claim *Mary Celeste* as salvage, but salvaged vessels were usually complete or partial wrecks left as a dead loss by their crew. *Mary Celeste* was a far cry from a wreck. She was a perfectly seaworthy ship whose cargo alone was insured for more than $36,000; she had, moreover, been abandoned without apparent reason.

The salvage hearings began on 18 December before Judge Sir James Cochrane and continued until 21 December, when the court was adjourned until after Christmas. On 23 December Morehouse ordered Deveau to take *Dei Gratia* on to Genoa and to deliver her cargo of petroleum. She arrived on 16 January.

Meanwhile, one of the most important characters in the *Mary Celeste* mystery began to play his hand. This was Frederick Solly Flood, a pompous, arrogant, excitable and very shrewd bureaucrat who gloried in the undeniably impressive title of Attorney General for Gibraltar and Advocate General for the Queen in Her Office of Admiralty. He found *Mary Celeste*'s abandonment beyond explanation and grew convinced that he was dealing with a case of mutiny or piracy and multiple murder. Without Solly Flood the mystery of *Mary Celeste* would have probably faded unmemorably into obscurity; instead, he focussed world attention on the proceedings in the Vice Admiralty Court – and out of it . . .

On 23 December Solly Flood dispatched a diver to inspect the vessel below the waterline while two carpenters, a shipwright, a timber expert and Mr John Austin, the Master Surveyor of Shipping, examined every rib and beam of the vessel in an effort to find a fault. The results were published in the *Gibraltar Chronicle* of 30 January 1873 and reprinted in *The Times* (London) on 14 February:

The result of this and a subsequent survey was, in brief, as
follows:- 1. As regards the cargo – it consisted of barrels
marked as containing alcohol, all of which were well stowed
and in good order and condition, except for one which had
been started. 2. As regards the exterior of the hull below
the waterline – it did not in any part exhibit the slightest
trace of damage, nor was there any appearance that the
vessel had come into collision with any other ship, nor that
she had struck on any ground or rock, nor, in short, that
she had sustained any injury whatever, the hull, the copper
with which it was covered, the stern, sternpost, and rudder
being all in good order and condition. 3. As regards the
interior of the ship – a very minute survey showed most
clearly that not only had the vessel not sustained any
accident, but that she could not have encountered any
seriously heavy weather. The whole of the hull, masts and
yards were in good condition, and the pitch in the water-
ways had not been started, which must have been the case
had any bad weather been experienced. The deck-house,
made of thin planking and six feet in height above the deck,
was perfect, there not being a crack in the planking nor
even in the paint. The seamans' chests and clothing found
on board were perfectly dry, some razors even being quite
free from rust. Moreover, a small phial containing oil for
use with a sewing machine was found in a perpendicular
position, which, together with a thimble and a reel of cotton
discovered near it, had not been upset, as must have been
the case if the ship had been subject to any stress of weather.
Spare panes of glass were also found stowed away and
unbroken. All the articles of furniture in the captain's
cabin, including a harmonium, were in their proper places
and uninjured by water, the music and other books also
being dry. Finally, the conclusion reached by Mr Austin,
the surveyor, is that there exists no apparent reason why
the vessel should have been abandoned. But, in addition
to the above facts, a sword was discovered which, on being
drawn out of its scabbard, exhibited signs of having been
smeared with blood and afterwards wiped; further the top-
gallant rail had marks on it, apparently of blood, and both
bows of the vessel had been cut, to all appearances inten-
tionally, with some sharp instrument.*

The results of Solly Flood's surveys revealed nothing beyond what was already known. However, the blood-stained sword and the blood stains on the deck and on the top-gallant rail suggested something very sinister to Flood and he was not slow in formulating a theory.

Flood's first idea was that *Mary Celeste*'s crew had gained access to the cargo of alcohol and had murdered Captain Briggs, his wife and child (and possibly Mate Richardson) in a drunken fury. Later, when sanity prevailed, they had thrown the bodies over the side, damaged the Celeste's hull to fake the appearance of an accident and had then fled in the yawl, hoping to reach Santa Maria and from there a safe port in the West Indies or South America. It was a good theory but flawed by the fact that the cargo was commercial alcohol, liable to give the drinker chronic pain long before intoxication set in.†

Flood's second theory featured Captain Briggs and Captain Morehouse in the role of conspirators. Briggs, with the possible assistance of Richardson, is seen as murdering his crew, disposing of the bodies over the side, and then fleeing to a destination prearranged with Captain Morehouse. *Dei Gratia* would find *Mary Celeste*, claim her as salvage, accept a handsome sum and then split it with Briggs. Again the theory is not without certain merits, but Briggs was not the sort of man to commit such a crime, nor is there any evidence that Morehouse or any of his crew would be a party to it. Moreover, Briggs, a part-owner of the ship, had a financial investment tied up in the vessel which was greater than what he could have expected to get as his share of the salvage money. Again Flood abandoned his idea.

*These marks on the hull have never been explained to everybody's satisfaction. A narrow strip about two to three feet above the waterline, about three eighths of an inch deep, one and a quarter inches wide, and about six or seven feet long, had been gouged from one of the outer planks. The damage was recent, done with a sharp cutting instrument and apparently intentional. Also, on the top-gallant rail near the bloodstains there was a deep cut which looked as if it could have been made with an axe *or a sword.*

†Solly Flood jumped to this theory before he had examined the full facts and his precipitate behaviour made him look a fool, but in this he was not alone. The same theory was advanced on 23 March 1873, long after Flood had discarded it, by William A. Richard, the then Secretary of the Treasury of the United States, in an open letter published on the front page of the *New York Times.*

Flood's third theory is not so easy to dismiss. He asserted that *Mary Celeste* must have been abandoned shortly after 25 November, the date of the last entry in the log. However, according to the crew of *Dei Gratia*, they first saw *Mary Celeste* on 5 December, some ten days later. At this time *Mary Celeste* was 500 miles beyond the position recorded in the log and had headed in the general direction of her intended destination. How was it possible, asked Flood, for an unmanned ship with a free wheel to hold her general course for ten days and cover 500 miles?

Flood further argued that the blood-stained sword, blood stains on the deck and top-gallant rail and the cut on the top-gallant rail were indications of violence. The absence of Captain Briggs, his family and crew suggested that they had been murdered. The murderers must have stood to gain by their crime and, since everything known to be aboard *Mary Celeste* was present, the only gain was the salvage reward; thus the murderers must be the captain and crew of *Dei Gratia*. As a theory it had merits, but as a case against Morehouse and his men it depended largely upon generating an atmosphere of suspicion in which Morehouse and the crew would be considered guilty until they could prove themselves innocent. Fortunately the Vice Admiralty Court was not to fall for such a flagrant abuse of the law, and cleared Morehouse and his crew of any suspicion. The Court issued its verdict on 14 March 1873. On Friday 28 March 1873 *The Times* (London) reported:

> In the Vice Admiralty Court at Gibraltar on the 14th Inst., the Hon. the Chief Justice gave judgement in the *Mary Celeste* salvage case and awarded the sum of £1,700 to the master and crew of the Nova Scotian brigantine *Dei Gratia* for the salvage services rendered by them; the costs of the suit to be paid out of the property salved. The *Mary Celeste* was valued at $5,700 and her cargo at $36,943 – total $42,643, so the award may be set down as one-fifth of the total value.

In the opinion of many people the award should have been almost three times as much.

Mary Celeste was returned to James H. Winchester and

entrusted to the care of Captain George W. Blatchford, a new skipper brought from New York to take the vessel on to Genoa. Despite some initial trouble in finding men to form a crew, Blatchford arrived in Genoa on 21 March and delivered the cargo of commercial alcohol to H. Mascarhenas and Co.

Winchester then sold *Mary Celeste*. It is said that he sold her as soon as he had found a buyer – some say that he even made a loss from the deal – but that doesn't seem in character with the semi-illiterate, hard-swearing and tough-minded businessman that we know Winchester to have been.

Over the next twelve years *Mary Celeste* changed hands no less than seventeen times. None of her owners was lucky with her: on a voyage to Montevideo she lost most of her cargo and rigging in a storm; on another occasion her cargo of horses and mules died, shortly followed by her skipper. She spent twelve months rotting on a wharf in the Eeri Basin. The rest of her time was spent with the American Coastal Service, lurching up and down the coast losing cargoes, sails and sailors, running aground and catching fire with depressing regularity. Then, in late 1884, *Mary Celeste* passed into the hands of a consortium from Boston, the principal owner being sixty-one-year-old Gilman C. Parker, a sea-shark who hailed from Winthrop, Massachusetts. He loaded the vessel with a cargo of ale, boots, shoes, bread, butter, beef, codfish, furniture and other items, all of which he insured for $30,000 as first-class merchandise: the cargo, even in the event that it included the items he claimed, was in fact of poor quality and worth no more than a few hundred dollars. Parker then sailed for the Gulf of Gonave, near Mirageone, Haiti, a narrow bay divided into two channels by the Isle de la Gonave. In the middle of the southern channel lay a row of razor-like coral teeth known as Rochaelais Bank. It was here, on 3 January 1885 that Parker deliberately ran *Mary Celeste* aground.

He unloaded everything saleable, poured petrol over the ship's deck and set the vessel alight. The *Mary Celeste* burned well and by evening nothing remained but her charred ribs. *Mary Celeste* died in the most wretched circumstances that can befall a ship, but the jinx that had bedevilled her was not exorcised by the flames – as Parker and his associates were about to find out!

Parker sold *Mary Celeste*'s cargo for $500 to a certain Mr

Mitchell, the United States Consul in Haiti, and returned with
his associates to Boston, where he filed a salvage claim. For
some reason the insurance companies were suspicious and
decided to investigate, hiring two insurance investigators, Mr
Kingman Putnam, a brother of the founder of the famous
publishing business, and Henry M. Rogers, who happened to
be in Haiti investigating the loss of a schooner off the south
coast. It was not long before the truth was discovered and
orders issued for the arrest of all concerned.

Parker and three associates were arrested and sent for trial
in a Federal Court charged with barratry (wilful negligence),
a crime punishable by death. However, a legal technicality
prevented the course of justice and they walked from the
court free men – free from the justice of man, but not from
the jinx of *Mary Celeste*: one of the conspirators went mad
and was placed in a mental institution; another committed
suicide; Parker died in poverty and disrepute; the companies
involved in the swindle went bankrupt; and, as for Mr Mitchell,
the man who bought *Mary Celeste*'s cargo, he disappeared as
soon as he heard that he was wanted for his part in the
conspiracy. The President of Haiti offered to put soldiers on
his trail, to capture him and force him to board the British
steamer *Saxon*, where he could be arrested by Mr Putnam,
who would have to disguise himself as the ship's chaplain
because *Saxon* was not allowed to carry passengers. Putnam
declined, uncertain of the complications which might arise
from the abduction of an American citizen from Haitian
territory by a fraudulent man of God illegally aboard a British
ship. As far as we know Mitchell escaped justice, although his
actual fate remains unknown. Ironically, the British ship
Saxon was later wrecked with loss of life.

Having read this account of *Mary Celeste* you may be
wondering about the omission of what would seem the most
striking details of the story: the breakfast cooking in the
galley; the all-important page missing from the log; the mugs
of warm tea on the galley table; the aroma of fresh tobacco
smoke lingering in the captain's cabin. In fact these melo-
dramatic details are pure fiction. The *Mary Celeste* myth really
began in January 1884, some eleven months before she was
run aground, when the *Cornhill Magazine*, one of the most

respected journals of its day, published a tale called 'J. Habakuk Jephson's Statement'. It appeared anonymously because its author was a practising doctor and prevented from using his name by professional etiquette. It was, in fact, one of the first literary attempts of a young writer named Arthur Conan Doyle.

Doyle never intended that his story be taken for anything more than a piece of fiction and 'J. Habakuk Jephson's Statement' was full of so many glaring errors that nobody in possession of the true facts should have thought otherwise. In Doyle's story *Mary Celeste*'s skipper is a genial New Englander named Tibbs and is far too ineffectual to resemble Captain Briggs; the crew is different from the actual crew; and Doyle's *Celeste* bears no resemblance to the actual vessel. Doyle also started a tradition by erroneously calling the ship *Marie Celeste*, a mistake that is said to have first been made in *Lloyd's List* of 25 March 1873. However, despite these errors, Doyle's blood-drenched drama was published in several American newspapers as a factual reconstruction of the mystery, and both Consul Horatio Sprague and Solly Flood were moved to write letters condemning the tale and its author.

The most outrageous 'factual' account of the *Mary Celeste* mystery appeared in the late 1920s in an article by Lee Kaye in *Chambers' Journal*. It was later expanded in a book by Laurence J. Keating, *The Great Mary Celeste Hoax*, which was published in 1929. Of this book Keating said: '. . . the purpose of this present narrative is to put on record an exact and accurate account of what really did happen on board the vessel during her famous and magical voyage, to explain how and why she was abandoned, and to reveal what became of her crew.' Keating therefore left no doubt in his readers' minds that his book was anything but a true account. To make this point crystal clear, he continued: 'No evidence has been included which has not been investigated and corroborated; no document is quoted which has not been examined. The history is placed before the reader complete and accurate in all respects.'

According to Keating, Captain Briggs was an ineffectual skipper and dominated by his hulking, bullying Mate, Toby Jackson Hullock. The cook was a callow youth of eighteen years named John Pemberton, and the crew, three of whom were *Dei Gratia* men lent to Briggs, were a bunch of disreputable near-pirates.

To cut a long story short, during a violent storm Mrs Briggs' piano is wrenched free of its moorings and falls upon the helpless woman, crushing her to death. She is buried at sea, contrary to Captain Briggs' wishes, and, bereft with grief, he throws himself over the side. A short time later, following a brawl with Mate Hullock, a seaman named Venholdt either jumps or is thrown over the side and drowned. The crew, although innocent of causing the deaths, realise that their bad reputations will work against them in court and they decide to abandon ship; all, that is, except for the three men loaned to Captain Briggs from *Dei Gratia* and John Pemberton, the cook. They are subsequently rescued by *Dei Gratia* and tell their story to Captain Morehouse, who immediately seizes the chance of taking *Mary Celeste* into Gibraltar and claiming her as salvage.

Years later the cook, John Pemberton, who had been persuaded to keep his mouth shut at the time, decided to reveal all, telling his story first to Lee Kaye and later to Laurence Keating, whose book became a best-seller on both sides of the Atlantic. But John Pemberton proved as elusive as the Scarlet Pimpernel until an industrious 'special correspondent' of the London *Evening Standard* finally tracked him down and published an interview and a photograph of Pemberton, then an old man of eighty-two, in the *Evening Standard* of 6 May 1929.

The Great Mary Celeste Hoax was a hoax and it very nearly fooled the world. John Pemberton did not exist and the whole thing was the invention of Keating, a Liverpool-Irishman who also wrote the *Chambers' Journal* article as Lee Kaye and the *Evening Standard* piece, the photograph of Pemberton being a photograph of Keating's own father. One can only marvel at his effrontery and wish that Solly Flood had been alive in the 1920s. Perhaps the best comment on *The Great Mary Celeste Hoax* was made by Charles Edey Fay, a noted authority on the *Celeste* mystery, who wrote:

> *Here lies a book, of which it may be said*
> *It hoaxed the living and defamed the dead.*

Many reasonable theories have, of course, been put forward over the years, the most reasonable suggesting that the cargo of alcohol gave off fumes that either resulted in a minor explosion in the hold or that an explosion seemed probable. Captain Briggs panicked, fearing for his wife and child, and abandoned ship, possibly securing the yawl to *Mary Celeste* with the main peak halyard. This rope subsequently became free of *Mary Celeste* and the small, overloaded yawl was left to the mercy of the stormy sea. In either case however it would be a singular situation for fumes or an explosion to have left no evidence or vestige of damage. Gershom Bradford, author of *The Secret of Mary Celeste*, has also questioned the possibility that the cargo would have given off dangerous fumes in the first place. The cargo is said to have been nine barrels 'missing'; the precise meaning of 'missing' is unclear however. It could mean that the consignment was nine barrels short, that nine barrels had leaked during the journey, or that the total leakage from all 1,700 barrels was the equivalent of nine barrels. In Mr Bradford's opinion, a leakage would not have caused a problem. The alcohol would have found its way into the bilges, where it would have been diluted by the bilgewater and eventually discharged into the sea when the *Celeste* was pumped each morning. However, there would have been dramatic results if the alcohol had given off fumes. Mr Bradford gave the known facts about the cargo to 'an authority on alcohol' whose opinion was that no visible vapours would have been produced in the conditions pertaining; this eliminates the suggestion that escaping fumes were mistaken for smoke. Alcohol fumes could have mixed with the air and formed an explosive mixture, however, and the fumes could have been ignited by a naked light during cargo inspection or even by the metal bands around the barrels rubbing against each other. But, said the expert, if such a mixture had formed and been ignited, there would never have been any doubt as to what had happened to the *Mary Celeste* – she would have been blown out of the water!

Captain Briggs' use of the main peak-halyard has also been questioned. The lazaretto hatch was uncovered, suggesting that somebody had gone below to fetch a coil of rope. On the other hand, Deveau said that the halyard was 'broke and gone'. The halyard would not have broken unless used for a purpose for which it was not intended, which does suggest that it could have been used instead of a new rope. However, its employment in the manner suggested is thought inconsistent with the evidence of a hurried evacuation. Captain Briggs and his crew left *Mary Celeste* with only the sextant, chronometer and ship's papers. They did not take food, fresh water or extra clothing, not even their pipes and tobacco. Yet in the midst of this hurried activity there sat a seaman patiently unreeving 200–300 feet of heavy rope through no less than five pulley systems. Some students of the mystery maintain that this would have been the work of but a few moments, but others say that it would have been a slow task under good conditions, the halyard having a tendency to foul unless unreeved with care, and certainly not an operation likely to be undertaken when the ship was expected to be blown sky-high at any moment.

Of all the many theories proposed to explain the abandonment of *Mary Celeste*, the most likely was offered in the Vice Admiralty Court by Oliver Deveau. When asked if he had an opinion as to the cause of the abandonment, Deveau replied that he was of the belief that there was panic 'from the belief that the vessel had more water than had afterwards proved'. This idea has not impressed many commentators and it is sometimes cited as evidence of Deveau's lack of intelligence, imagination or both. I don't subscribe to this at all. The future Captain Deveau was a seaman of proven skills, but he was a man of few words and did not go beyond answering the questions put to him. He did not elaborate on his theory and he was not asked to: it has been left to future investigators to interpret his reasoning.

The late Dr James H. Kimble, one-time head of the United States Weather Bureau in New York, and Gershom Bradford, author of *The Secret Of Mary Celeste*, have both suggested that the vessel was struck by a waterspout, the sea's equivalent of a tornado (twister), which raises a cone of spray from the surface into a huge column of whirling wind and water from 20 to over 200 feet in height. Waterspouts can be short or high, fat or thin, narrow or wide, slanting or erect, and may be either harmless at one extreme or extremely dangerous at the other. They are not always easy to see, can appear without warning and last for up to an hour before breaking up and disappearing. They are usually found in the tropics, but they can appear almost anywhere: in December 1920 the steamer *British Marquis* sighted no less than twenty 'spouts in the English Channel!

It is not an everyday occurrence for a ship to be struck by a waterspout, but it is not a rare event either. One of the most impressive tales of such a meeting was told by the survivors of the 1,600-ton *Wasatch*, which was sunk by a waterspout when homeward-bound from the Philippines. On the day of the disaster the sky was an endless blue except for a small black dot on the horizon. Nobody paid it much attention until it grew larger and was seen to be a gigantic waterspout. Evasive action was taken, but to no avail; the waterspout struck the *Wasatch* with tremendous force and the world vanished behind a deluge of blackish water which swept the captain, mate, and half the crew over the side. The nightmare was over in less than half a minute. The waterspout moved on, leaving a broken *Wasatch* in its wake.

Gershom Bradford believes that *Mary Celeste* was struck by a waterspout of less violence than this, and that Captain Briggs abandoned ship because neither he nor his crew were familiar with the peculiar characteristics of the waterspout: within a 'spout the barometric pressure is extremely low and, as the spout passed over the ship, it would have created a marked difference in pressure between the inside and outside of the hull. The pressure within the ship could have caused the hatch covers to blow off and to snap open the skylight in Briggs' cabin – the same effect causes a building's walls to explode outward when struck by a tornado. Wind-driven water would have then poured below deck, thus accounting for the water in the hold.

The drop in barometric pressure would also have driven the bilge water up the pump-well, where a valve in the lower box of the pump would have prevented the bilge water from returning to the hold after the waterspout had passed by. Thus, when the ship was sounded, it would have seemed as if she had leaked six to eight feet of water in less than a minute and was sinking rapidly.

'The weather records of the Azores Islands,' writes Bradford, 'reveal that a depression was passing to the northward of the

Mary Celeste and she, on November 14, was in the westerly winds of the semi-circle of this disturbance.' In other words, conditions were right for a waterspout and *Mary Celeste* was favourably positioned to meet one. Thus it is supposed that on 25 November a whirling waterspout was sighted to the windward and bearing down on *Mary Celeste*. Captain Briggs took evasive action, but his ship was engulfed by wild, noisy, roaring confusion. The sails were torn from the bolt-ropes and a deluge of swirling water crashed over the decks. The barometric pressure dropped, the small hatch covers flew off and the cabin skylight snapped open, and wind-driven water poured below. Then the danger passed, the spout moved on and a shaken, disorganised and confused crew was left in its wake. Captain Briggs instructed a seaman to sound the ship. The low barometric pressure had forced the bilge water up the pump-well, giving the impression that the ship was on the verge of sinking: Captain Briggs therefore gave the order to abandon ship.

The waterspout theory fits the circumstances as perfectly as any theory could and much better than most, but is it what actually happened? That we shall never know. The case of *Mary Celeste* is a perplexing mystery, a perfectly structured riddle. It is, as one commentator put it, 'a detective-story writer's nightmare: the perfectly perplexing situation without any logical solution – a plot which can never be convincingly unravelled'.

Mary Celeste was a jinxed ship cursed with misfortune. It would seem that Captain Briggs and his family were jinxed too:

Benjamin Briggs' father, Captain Nathan Briggs, survived years at sea only to be killed when struck by lightning as he stood in the doorway of his home.

Benjamin Briggs vanished from *Mary Celeste*.

Two of Benjamin's brothers died at sea of yellow fever, another was lost shipboard, and a sister was lost in a shipwreck.

Benjamin's son, Arthur Stanley, was listed as missing in Cuba in 1898. His body was never found.

Arthur's son (Benjamin's grandson), a Major Briggs, disappeared during the First World War.

'Major Briggs' son (Benjamin's great-grandson), a Navy captain named Franklin Briggs, disappeared near the Arctic Circle in 1955. He had flown out with two companions and did not come back. His aircraft was found a week later by Eskimos, but its occupants were never seen again.*

*The information about Benjamin's descendants comes from a booklet called *Mysterious Disappearances* by Kurt Glemser, whose source is the *Journal of Boderland Research* for June 1960. The *Journal*'s source is an article in the *Navy Times* of 10 December 1955.

9 Vanishing From the Skies

Flying is the safest way to travel, or so any airline PRO will tell you. Air safety is the primary concern of every airline. Air and ground staff are highly trained professionals, aircraft are precision-built machines and every flight is backed by the best of human technology. It is hardly surprising, therefore, that air disasters make newspaper headlines around the world and immediately become problems which aviation experts are determined to solve. However, the sky is the home of many mysteries.

Glenn Miller
Few disappearances have caused as much sorrow as the disappearance of the band leader Glenn Miller. Miller, who was exempt from active service because of age and bad eyesight, was chosen to lead the American Band of the Allied Expeditionary Force. The AEF Programme was launched by the BBC who in 1944 broadcast to the troops following the Normandy landings; many famous entertainers performed for the programme.

Miller and his musicians arrived in London shortly after D-Day and were billeted in Lower Sloane Street. Their first night was spent sheltering in a basement from the blitz, and the following morning the haggard, weary group were moved fifty miles from London to the comparative safety of Bedford. That night their accommodation in Lower Sloane Street received a direct hit from a bomb and was completely destroyed.

The Miller band's first broadcast for the AEF, on 9 July 1944, was followed by an arduous schedule of performances, but Miller promised the troops preparing to invade France that he would make a special Christmas Day broadcast from Paris if the Allies liberated the city. This required that he pre-record no less than 129 shows, a daunting task that he miraculously succeeded in performing by Friday, 13 December.

On 15 December Miller climbed into an American jeep and was driven to Twin Woods Farm where an airfield had been constructed in 1939.

It was foggy and the RAF advised Miller not to fly, but Colonel Norman Basselle, Miller's pilot, was convinced that they could reach Orly if they left immediately. So, clutching his briefcase, Miller climbed into a small Norseman utility 'plane and the aircraft's engine spluttered into life. The 'plane taxied down the runway, gathered speed and lifted. That was the last that anybody saw of Glenn Miller.

Two days later the band arrived in France and were shocked to discover that Miller had not arrived. Two weeks passed without news. The BBC were still broadcasting the pre-recorded shows and the United States authorities had suspended casualty lists until after Christmas, so the news that Miller was missing was not widely known, but as the special Christmas Day broadcast approached and hope of finding Miller dwindled, the authorities were forced to announce the sad news. The band broadcast as promised, but it was a melancholy event without the quiet, unassuming Miller who had proved to be the band's greatest asset.

Rumours began to circulate soon after the news that Miller was missing was revealed: it was whispered that the British had accidentally shot down his 'plane; that he was still alive but mutilated beyond recognition; that he was insane and locked away in an asylum; that he was an enemy agent; that he had defected. None of the rumours proved to be true, but perhaps it is a measure of the man that such rumours circulated in the first place. However, the circumstances of his disappearance were certainly unusual and deserving of comment. Why was it that nobody knew of Miller's disappearance until the band arrived in Paris? Why didn't anybody check to see if Miller had arrived at Orly? Why didn't Orly seek information when Miller failed to arrive? Indeed, was Orly informed of Miller's intended arrival and, if not, why not?

We may also wonder why Miller chose to fly that day. The flying conditions were unfavourable and the RAF had advised against making the flight. The Christmas Day broadcast was important to Miller, but it would not have been affected by a short delay – indeed, it would not have been affected by a delay of several days. Why, then, did he fly? Is it true, as has been suggested, that Miller's superiors had forbidden him to fly that day? Was his an unscheduled flight, which would explain Orly's silence?

We shall probably never know what made Miller fly that day, but it's not too difficult to guess his fate. The weather deteriorated that afternoon, the fog grew worse and in such conditions radio failure would be disastrous. Somewhere over the Channel the Norseman's wings may have iced up, or perhaps some other failure occurred, and the small 'plane plummeted into the freezing North Sea.

Footprints In The Sand

In his book *Wild Talents*, Charles Fort records the details of a fascinating disappearance reported in the *Sunday Express* of 21 and 28 September 1924, and the *Sunday News* of 15 March 1925.

On 24 July 1924, at a time of Arab hostility, two British aviators, Flight-Lieutenant W. T. Day and Pilot Officer D. R. Stewart, left British HQ on a routine reconnaissance flight. They did not return. A search party found their aircraft in good condition, with sufficient fuel in the tanks to fly it back to base, but of Day and Stewart . . . All that remained was a trail of footprints in the sand stretching some forty yards from the aircraft, then coming to a sudden stop. Searchers looked ahead, sideways and backwards, but the footprints did not resume.

A little less than a year later the mystery had not been solved, nor had anybody claimed the reward for information offered at the time.

The Disappearance That Never Was

A similar story is told by Frank Edwards, the late television and radio broadcaster and author of books about UFOs and things unexplained. In his entertaining book *Stranger Than Science* he says that if asked to cite the strangest case of disappearance he would 'unhesitatingly refer to a twin-engined Marine 'plane which crashed on the Tahoma Glacier in 1947'. Searchers apparently reached the aircraft and found ample evidence that none of those aboard could have survived the devastating crash, yet the bodies of all thirty-two people were absent. The authorities were lost for an explanation and offered a $5,000 reward for information leading to the recovery of the bodies. The bodies were never found and the money never claimed.

I know what happened to those bodies, but I don't think the US authorities would pay $5,000 dollars for the information. The Tahoma Glacier is one of about twenty-five glaciers on Mount Rainier, the highest mountain in the Cascade Range in the State of Washington. It was here, in December 1946 (not 1947 as Edwards states), that a giant C-46 'Commando' Marine Corps transport 'plane crashed more than 10,000 feet up the storm-shrouded west slope of the dangerous, crevasse-scored South Tahoma Glacier. Six months later, on Monday 18 July 1947, wreckage was found and the bodies were located, some embedded in the ice. A party of the Army's specially trained mountain troops from Fort Lewis and Camp Carson, Colorado, and a team of guides and National Park Service Rangers, went to the crash site and dismissed any idea of retrieving the bodies. Dangerous rock falls made the operation too hazardous to even consider and it was accordingly decided to hold a memorial service instead. This took place on 24 August 1947, in a wooded, sunlit glade at the 4,000-foot summit of Round Pass on Mount Rainier.

The story of how the wreckage and the bodies were found and of the decision to hold a memorial service was told in several copies of the Seattle *Post-Intelligencer* during August 1947. It remains to be seen how the story of the bodies being missing survived until 1959 when Edwards' book was published.

Cody, Adams and the berserk blimp

On 16 August 1942 Lieutenant Ernest E. Cody and Ensign Charles E. Adams of Airship Squadron 32 climbed into the gondola below the ponderous gas-filled bag of their L-8 airship and headed west out over the San Francisco Bay and the Golden Gate to patrol San Francisco Harbour and the approaches. It was a journey from which they would never return.

It was wartime, and daily patrols of the California coast near San Francisco by airships and surface craft were a routine precaution against the possibility that enemy submarines might try to sneak into the harbour and create havoc.

A light drizzle and patches of early morning fog drifted in from the sea when Cody and Adams climbed aboard their airship at 6.00am and lifted from Treasure Island Naval Base. Both men were experienced with airships. Cody was particularly experienced, having 500 flying hours as an airship pilot.

At 7.55am Cody radioed the control tower at Moffett Field, an important Naval Air Station near the small residential town of Almeda on an island in San Francisco Bay, and reported that he was taking the L-8 down to 300 feet to get a better look at a sizeable oil slick on the water about five miles east of the Farallon Islands.

As the L-8 descended, two small fishing boats and a couple of patrol boats in the area of the slick sped to a safe distance, fearing that the airship might drop a couple of depth charges. All eyes aboard those vessels were fixed on the L-8 and all eyes were witness to an extraordinary event. The airship circled the oil slick and began a slow descent to 300 feet. Then, as if pulled upward by some celestial puppeteer, the blimp soared away and vanished in the overcast sky.

At 8.05am the radio operator at Moffett Field tried to contact the blimp. There was no response. He alerted air-sea rescue and two search 'planes were soon in the sky, but were forced to stay above a thick layer of cloud which obscured the sea below. Apart from a very brief sighting, they had nothing to report.

Over two hours passed, then, at 10.30am, a Pan-American clipper saw the airship to the south of the Golden Gate. Ten minutes later a search 'plane reported that the blimp had made a brief appearance above the overcast at 2,000 feet. Fifteen minutes later observers at Fort Funston, a Coast Artillery Patrol Station, saw the L-8 drifting towards a beach about a mile from their position. Two fishermen later reported that the blimp had struck the beach. They had grabbed the tie-lines but an inopportune gust of wind had lifted the airship and carried it – along with the two fishermen valiantly clinging to the tie-lines – for about 100 yards across the beach, eventually lifting it to a height at which the fishermen considered it prudent to let go. The L-8 sailed over the sands and struck a cliff, receiving a slight tear in the gas-bag. The impact also dislodged one of the 300 pound depth bombs, which buried itself in a nearby highway. Relieved of this weight, the blimp sailed away.

At 11.15am the L-8 appeared in the sky over Daly City to the south of San Francisco. It slowly descended and finally came to rest in the middle of a street. A Naval Salvage crew raced to the downed airship. There was still a little gas in the L-8's bag, the radio functioned properly, the parachutes and life rafts were safely stowed in place, and a check of the cavity below the deck of the gondola revealed that the airship had not touched water. The only things missing were two bright yellow life jackets, and Cody and Adams.

It was mandatory that life jackets be worn during overwater flights, so Cody and Adams must have been wearing them when they disappeared; but where had Cody and Adams gone? Investigators listened to the testimony of all the witnesses. The men in the fishing and patrol boats said that the blimp had descended to about 300 feet above the oil slick and then soared upwards and disappeared. They had not seen anything fall from the airship. The fishermen on the beach said that the gondola's door was open and that the gondola was empty.

Whatever fate befell Cody and Adams it must have happened during the L-8's uncharted 2-hour 55-minute journey between soaring away from the oil slick and hitting the beach, and the obvious solution is that the two men fell from the blimp. But how? And why?

The mystery deepens because, although the motors had stopped when the blimp was found in Daly City, one throttle was open, the other was half open, and the ignition switches were turned on. This suggests that Cody was secure in his seat and piloting the L-8 when he vanished!

One suggestion is that Adams was in danger of falling and that Cody went to his assistance, that there was a tangle and both men fell. However, it is believed that Cody would not have left the controls before reducing the engines, the act of a moment and instinct.

There was a prolonged and intensive search. At the end of the war enemy records were checked, but they did not mention Cody and Adams. The two men had vanished.

If the facts of this case are as given here, I would say that Cody and Adams must have fallen from the L-8 as it descended over the oil slick. Had they still been aboard at 8.05am they would have responded to the radio call from Moffett Field. Also, when relieved of their weight, the airship would have soared upwards, which is exactly what it did. It was almost 8.00am and the sky was overcast and misty. It was raining and patches of fog were drifting in from the sea. It is now impossible to say how well those aboard the fishing boats and patrol boats could have seen over the distance and in the conditions pertaining, but it is quite likely that they were unable to see the two, tiny yellow-clad figures plummet 300 feet into the sea.

The life jackets should have kept the men afloat or, if ripped from their bodies, would have floated on the sea to be found by searchers. But how long would it have taken for the tide to carry the bodies or life jackets from the scene of the oil slick and on out to sea?

On the available information I am inclined to believe that Cody and Adams fell from the blimp when it was over the oil slick and that the witnesses were too far away to see them; that in the hours which passed before a full-scale search was launched the sea carried the bodies far from the scene of the accident and eventually beyond the search area. However, maybe this explanation is too simple. The Navy apparently examined every possible explanation and drew a blank, filing the story of Cody, Adams and the berserk blimp as an unsolved mystery. I feel certain that my theory must have been considered, so perhaps the mystery is truly inexplicable.

The Man Who Vanished In Thin Air – Literally!
In the summer of 1968, twenty-three passengers boarded a Purdue Aviation Corporation chartered DC-3 airliner at Kankakee, Illinois, bound for a Lions Club convention in Dallas, Texas. 55-year-old insurance executive Jerrold I. Potter and his wife Carrie settled themselves in their seats towards the rear of the aircraft and relaxed.

Jerrold I. Potter was an affable, happy man who enjoyed life to the full. He was happily married, had two married daughters, and lived in a fine home in Pontiac. He was successful in business and had many good friends. He belonged to the Lions, the Moose, the Elks and the Chamber of Commerce. He was in good health and untroubled by worries of a nature other than those which are accepted as an unavoidable feature of ordinary life. In short, Jerrold I. Potter was not the sort of man one would select to play the feature rôle in a bizarre mystery.

After about an hour, when the DC-3 was to the north of Rolla, Missouri, and approaching Fort Leonard Wood camp, Potter decided to go to the lavatory. This was near the exit door at the tail of the aircraft. On the way Potter stopped to chat with a friend, James Schaive, president of the Ottowa, Illinois, Lions Club. They chatted for a few moments and then Potter continued on his way to the lavatory.

A few minutes later there was a brief moment of turbulence. The 'plane quivered but soon recovered.

Time passed and Potter did not return to his seat. His wife began to grow uneasy and eventually called for a stewardess. Would she be so kind as to check the lavatory and see if her husband was still there and had not been taken sick. The stewardess went to fulfil the request.

Meanwhile, the pilot, Miguel Raul Cabeza, noticed that a red warning light on the control panel had flashed 'on', indicating that the rear exit door was open. He asked the co-pilot, Roy Bacus, to go back and check.

Co-pilot Bacus was making his way down the aisle towards the rear of the 'plane when he met the stewardess coming towards the pilot's compartment. They exchanged a few hurried words and made their way to the rear of the 'plane.

The lavatory was unoccupied and the exit door was open. Jerrold I. Potter had not returned to his seat!

There are three possible solutions: Potter deliberately opened the exit door and jumped 8,000 feet to his death; he mistook the exit door for the door to the lavatory and was sucked out by the slipstream; or the door had not been fastened properly before take-off and opened when Potter may have been thrown against it by the sudden bout of turbulence.

Friends and relatives said that Potter had no reason to kill himself. However, psychiatrists are aware of a condition known as 'smiling depression'. A severely depressed person suffering thus may behave quite normally and display no evidence of his depression while involved in the daily routine, but in a moment of silent inactivity he can become aware of his despair and kill himself. Was Jerrold Potter a 'smiling suicide'? His family and friends did not believe that he was and, so far as I am aware, there is no evidence to suggest otherwise; therefore, with a few reservations, the first solution can be eliminated.

It is possible that Potter mistook the exit door for the door to the lavatory. Such a mistake would be remarkable – not to say extraordinary – but it is one for which there is a precedent. Almost forty years to the month earlier Alfred Lowenstein, a multimillionaire and one of the richest men in Europe, boarded his private Amsterdam-built Fokker VII for a short cross-channel flight. He was seen to leave his seat, walk to the rear of the aircraft and step into the lavatory compartment. He was never seen again. Investigators found that the exit door, which was in the lavatory compartment, was slightly open. Murder was eliminated and all the people who knew the tough-minded and often ruthless businessman were adamant in their conviction that suicide was inconsistent with Lowenstein's character. Thus the only reasonable explanation was that Lowenstein, engrossed in business matters as usual, had mistaken the exit door for the door to the lavatory. He pushed against it and it resisted. Characteristically, he threw his weight against the door and it opened about two feet. Lowenstein lost his balance and was dragged out by the slipstream.

Did a similar event occur in 1968?

There are differences. Lowenstein's aircraft was his own. The DC-3 upon which Potter was travelling was a public airliner and the airline which owned it had taken every pre-caution to guard against anybody opening wrong doors. The DC-3's exit door bore the words 'DO NOT OPEN WHILE IN FLIGHT' stencilled in large white letters on a red background. It was hinged at the top, which would have been most unusual for a door to a lavatory. It was secured with a safety chain and it could only be opened if a handle was turned 180 degrees to release two plunger bolts. Moreover, even if Potter had ignored the warning, released the safety chain and turned the handle 180 degrees, it would still have taken a determined effort to open the door while the aircraft was in flight.

Finally, could Potter have been thrown against the exit door, which had not been fastened properly? Again there is a precedent. In 1950 Marc Fischer-Galati, a steward on a DC-3 belonging to Eastern Airlines, was thrown against the exit door, which had not been fastened properly, and plunged out of the aircraft. He survived; a piece of safety chain coiled around his right leg and he also managed to hold onto the door handle. He was miraculously still gripping the handle when the DC-3 descended 2,500 feet and landed at Miami Airport! However, investigations revealed that on Mr Potter's flight the exit door had been securely locked before take-off and Mr Grove Webster, president of Purdue Aviation, said that the doors of DC-3 aircraft were very difficult to open even when the aircraft was on the ground; the stewardesses usually had to have the door opened and closed for them by a male member of the crew. It was also pointed out that the DC-3 was not pressurised and that a person could stand in the open doorway and not be sucked out.

Thus all the possible explanations seem far too remote to be considered probable. All we can say for certain is that Jerrold I. Potter vanished in thin air – literally!

10 Flight 19

First, the generally accepted account:

At two o'clock in the afternoon of 5 December 1945 five Avenger torpedo bombers roared from the runway at Fort Lauderdale Naval Air Station, Florida, and set course on a routine training exercise which would take them on a triangular flight over the Bermuda Triangle. With the exception of one aircraft, each 'plane carried a crew of three, a total of fourteen highly experienced airmen.

At 3.45 the radio operator in the control tower at Fort Lauderdale received the first word from the 'planes, designated Flight 19, but instead of the expected request for landing instructions, he received an urgent message from the flight leader, a young lieutenant named Charles Carrol Taylor: 'Calling tower, this is an emergency. We seem to be off course. We cannot see land . . . repeat . . . we cannot see land!'

'What is your position?' radioed the tower.

'We are not sure of our position. We can't be sure just where we are. We seem to be lost.'

'Assume bearing due west.'

'We . . . we don't know which way is west,' replied Taylor, sounding worried, confused, and perhaps frightened. 'Everything is wrong . . . strange. We can't be sure just where we are. We're not sure of any direction. Even the ocean doesn't look as it should.'

Contact with Lt Taylor suddenly ceased and for several minutes the hiss of static filled the Lauderdale control tower. When Flight 19 came through again Lt Taylor was no longer in command.

'We can't tell where we are . . . we must be . . . everything's . . . can't make out anything.' There was no forced courage in this man's voice: he was terrified, and the words

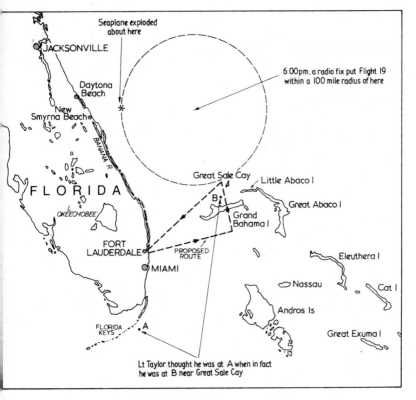

Flight 19 – where they actually were and where Lieutenant Taylor thought they were. His confusion created the precarious position in which the aircraft found themselves.

that followed were no more than the ramblings of a man close to hysteria. The tower personnel looked at each other in bewilderment. What the hell was going on out there? Again Flight 19 contacted the tower: 'Not certain of where we are . . . we think we're 225 miles northeast of base . . . it looks like we are entering . . .' The voice broke off and there was silence.

Meanwhile, Lt Robert Cox, the senior flight instructor at Fort Lauderdale, circling the runway of the Naval Air Station preparing to land, had overheard the bewildering series of messages and thought he had a vague idea where Flight 19 might be. He radioed: 'Flight 19, what is your altitude? I'll fly south and meet you.'

After a few minutes silence Lt Taylor exclaimed: 'Don't come after me. It looks . . .'

Not another word was heard from the five bombers.

The time was now about 4.30. The Lauderdale tower declared an emergency and within minutes a huge flying boat was heading towards Flight 19's last estimated position. A few minutes later the tower tried to contact the seaplane for a position report. There was no answer. Further attempts to raise the aircraft also failed. The flying boat had followed Flight 19 into oblivion.

Almost 250,000 square miles of sea and coastline were searched in what was then the largest air-sea rescue operation in history. Scores of ships and aircraft combed the entire region for some trace of wreckage or debris, but nothing was found. Flight 19 and the flying boat had vanished in the true tradition of the Bermuda Triangle – no wreckage, no debris, no bodies, no survivors.

'They vanished as completely as if they had flown to Mars,' said one Navy officer. 'This unprecedented peacetime loss seems to be a total mystery, the strangest ever investigated in the annals of naval aviation,' said another.

Rumours soon began to circulate. It was said that Lt Taylor had said much more than was generally known, that he had said something that was top secret.

The Navy conducted a secret inquiry in Miami and issued a report, but it turned out to be difficult to get at it. One man was determined to solve the mystery: one-time newsman Art Ford. He kept chipping away at the story, gathering one fact here and another there until a picture emerged. He talked to civilian radio operators and found some who had actually overheard some of the transmissions between Flight 19 and the control tower. One ham in Florida had something incredible to say. He claimed to have overheard the last message from Lt Taylor. He said the last words had been: 'Don't come after me. They look like they're from outer space.'

There was no way to confirm that this was in fact what Lt Taylor had said, but it would explain a great deal. It would explain why Taylor refused assistance; why he was terrified; why the aircraft vanished: Taylor and the crew of Flight 19 had encountered something beyond their experience, something beyond the experience of most human beings.

Flight 19, the Lost Patrol, is the cornerstone of the Bermuda
Triangle legend. In fact, it was because of Flight 19 that
many people began to take a closer look at the disappearances in that region. Every book and article about this
patch of ocean quotes the messages between Flight 19 and
Lauderdale tower and, if repetition can be considered a guide
to truth, there can be no doubt that Flight 19 is the most
astounding mystery in the annals of aviation. However, it
may not come as any great surprise to learn that repetition is
not a guide to truth and that the true facts of what happened
that day have been distorted to make the event look far more
mysterious than it ever really was.

The report of the official inquiry is a hefty document of
about 400 pages. From it and other reliable sources it is
possible to learn what happened that chilly December afternoon in 1945.

At one o'clock on 5 December, thirteen student airmen
assembled inside the training office at Fort Lauderdale for a
pre-flight briefing from Lt Taylor. There should have been
fourteen students – the TBM Avengers normally carried a
crew of three: a pilot, a gunner and a radioman – but on this
particular day marine gunner, Corporal Allen Kosnar had
asked to be excused duty. Twenty-four years later, when he
returned to Fort Lauderdale to participate in a documentary
film, *The Devil's Triangle*, he explained that he had had a
premonition not to fly.

Lt Taylor was fifteen minutes late and did not arrive at
the training office until 1.15, which meant that take-off had
to be delayed until two o'clock. He apologised, but did not
offer any explanation, and said that he did not want to take
Flight 19 out. He asked the aviation training duty officer,
Lt Arthur A. Curtis, to find another instructor to take his
place, but no relief was available and Lt Curtis had to refuse
the request. Taylor had given no explanation for the request
and it has since been suggested that he was either sick or
drunk. Lt Curtis, however, told the Board of Inquiry that
Taylor did not behave abnormally and the navy established
that he was in a satisfactory condition to fly. Indeed, in
October 1947 a page was added to the report absolving
Taylor of any blame for the loss of the aircraft.

The fourteen men gathered in the training office were not

'highly experienced', as the Triangle legend would have us believe. With the exception of Lt Taylor, they had about 350–400 flying hours to their credit, only 55 hours of which had been in TBM-type aircraft. Lt Taylor was the most experienced flyer among them, being a combat veteran with 2,509 hours, but he had spent the last six months at the Miami Naval Air Station and had never flown the route to be taken by Flight 19 that day.

Moreover, the flight was not 'routine'. It was a navigation problem: fly east (091 degrees) for 56 miles and conduct practice low-level bombing at Hens and Chickens Shoals; continue on course for 67 miles; turn northward (346 degrees) for 73 miles; turn west-southwest (241 degrees) for just over 120 miles back to base. In short, a triangular flight within the Bermuda Triangle.

The weather was about average for a flight of this kind: scattered rain showers within which the ceiling was about 2,500 feet, visibility 6–8 miles; unlimited ceiling outside the showers, visibility 10–12 miles; surface winds between 20 and 31 knots; sea moderate to rough. Not exactly 'perfect' flying conditions.

Flight 19 roared from the runway and set course for the first leg of the flight. There had been a thorough pre-flight check of the aircraft and everything was in perfect working order. The flight was expected to take about two hours and each of the five aircraft carried about five and a half hours of fuel. However, it would appear that none of the aircraft had a clock and none of the crew had a watch. Flight 19 was therefore flying without any means of knowing the time, something that would naturally lead to disorientation.

A few minutes after 2.30 Lauderdale tower overheard an inter-aircraft communication. 'I've got one more bomb to drop,' somebody said. 'Go ahead and drop it,' came the reply. It was at about this time that the skipper of a fishing boat working near Hens and Chickens Shoals saw several aircraft flying east.

Flight 19 carried out the bombing according to plan and continued east for about 67 miles. It would seem that at about this point things began to go wrong. The five 'planes turned north for the second leg of the flight.

At about 3.40 Lt Cox was circling the Lauderdale runway

when he overheard a radio communication. A voice was asking someone (or something) called 'Powers' what his compass read.

'I don't know where we are,' replied Powers. 'We must have got lost after that last turn.'

Lt Cox radioed Lauderale tower: 'I've got a 'plane or a boat which answers to "Powers" which seems to be in trouble.' He then radioed on 'Powers'' frequency: 'This is FT-74 (Cox's call sign). Boat or 'plane calling "Powers" please identify yourself so someone can help you.'

There was no immediate response, but a few moments later the ship or boat calling 'Powers' asked: 'Does anyone have any suggestions?'

Lt Cox did not know that 'Powers' was Captain Edward Joseph Powers, Jnr., a pilot of one of the TBMs in Flight 19. He radioed: 'This is FT-74. Boat or ship calling "Powers", what is your trouble?'

'FT-74, this is FT-28,' came the reply. 'Both my compasses are out. I'm trying to find Fort Lauderdale, Florida. I'm over land but it's broken. I'm sure I'm in the Keys but I don't know how far down and I don't know how to get to Fort Lauderdale.'

Lt Taylor's compasses were not working and he was lost. He thought he was over familiar territory, somewhere over the Florida Keys, a chain of small islands which curve out about 100 miles from South Florida into the Gulf of Mexico. In reality, Flight 19 was probably north of Great Sale Cay in the northern Bahamas, which looks remarkably similar to the Keys from the air.

'FT-28, this is FT-74. Put the sun on your port wing if you are in the Keys and fly up the coast until you get to Miami. Fort Lauderdale is twenty miles further, your first port after Miami. The air station is directly on your left from the port. What is your present altitude? I'll fly south and meet you.'

'FT-74, this is FT-28. I know where I am now. I'm at 2,300 feet. Don't come after me.'

Lt Taylor's instruction, 'Don't come after me', is obviously the comment allegedly overheard by the Florida radio ham: however, there is no mention of anything that looked like it had come from outer space.

'FT-28, this is FT-74. Roger. You're at 2,300 feet. I'm coming to meet you anyhow.'

A few minutes passed in silence, then Taylor radioed: 'FT-74, this is FT-28. We have just passed over a small island. We have no other land in sight. Can you have Miami or someone turn on their radar gear and pick us up? We don't seem to be getting far. We were out on a navigation hop and on the second leg. I thought they were going wrong so I took over and was flying them back to their right position, but I'm sure now that neither of my compasses are working.'

'You can't expect to get here in ten minutes,' replied Cox. 'You have a thirty to thirty-five knot head- or crosswind. Turn on your IFF gear. Or do you have it on?'

The IFF gear would brighten Flight 19's image on the radar screen. Taylor had not switched it on. Cox also told him to turn on the ZBX equipment, an instrument which 'homes' on the home base and tells the pilot in which direction to fly.

A few minutes later Flight 19's transmissions began to fade; then Lt Cox's transmitter failed and he was no longer able to contact Taylor. He tried to raise Flight 19 on all five VHF frequencies but without success. However, he could still hear Taylor and at about four o'clock he heard somebody say that visibility was between ten and fifteen miles. Twenty-five minutes later, Port Everglades, the Lauderdale Air-Sea Rescue Task Force station, established contact with Taylor. 'I'm at Angels 3.5,' he told them, meaning that he was at 3,500 feet. 'Have on emergency IFF. Does anyone in the area have a radar screen that could pick us up?'

'Roger FT-28. Stand by.'

Port Everglades did not have any direction-finding equipment but they passed the message to Fort Lauderdale and received a promise that the Miami Naval Air Station would be informed of the request. In fact a total of twenty land bases were contacted and asked to assist in locating Flight 19 and several coast guard vessels were prepared for action. Unfortunately there was a breakdown in the teletype communications and Cuban radio broadcasts were hampering radio fixes.

'FT-28. We suggest that you have another 'plane in your

flight with a good compass take over the lead and guide you back to the mainland,' radioed Port Everglades.

'Roger.'

Lt Taylor definitely agreed to Port Everglades' logical solution to Flight 19's predicament, but for some reason he did not relinquish control.

At 4.30, the time at which most accounts of the loss claim that Fort Lauderdale received the last word from Flight 19, Lt Taylor contacted Port Everglades: 'One of the 'planes in the flight thinks if we went 270 degrees we could hit land.'

Taylor did not take this advice. Fifteen minutes later he said: 'We'll head 030 degrees for forty-five minutes, then we'll fly north to make sure we're not over the Gulf of Mexico.'

Meanwhile, Lt Cox had landed at Fort Lauderdale and gone to the operations room where he asked the duty officer for permission to take out the one-man Ready 'Plane. Cox later told the Board of Inquiry: 'I thought I'd fly up to the northeast section to see if I could pick up Flight 19's transmissions.' He didn't get a definite answer from the duty officer, 'so I went up to the tower and Lieutenant-Commander Poole, the flight officer, was up there. I asked him about taking the Ready 'Plane out and he said very definitely "no". He didn't think that there was any use in taking it out then.'

Actually Lt-Commander Poole already had a man waiting in the Ready 'Plane, but he didn't know in which direction to send it. His decision not to send the 'plane out was therefore correct but, in retrospect, it was unfortunate; Lt Cox was certain that Flight 19 was not over the Florida Keys and had he been permitted to play his hunch it is probable that he would have found the lost aircraft.

So far, every attempt to locate Flight 19 had failed. Port Everglades asked Taylor to switch his radio frequency to the search-and-rescue channel, which was undisturbed by the Cuban radio broadcasts and could be received by many stations unable to get the flight's training frequency. Unfortunately Taylor refused: 'I can't change frequencies,' he said. 'I must keep my 'planes together.'

About five o'clock Lt Taylor announced: 'Change course to 090 degrees for ten minutes.'

A few minutes later one of the students exclaimed: 'Dammit! If we would just fly west we would get home. Head west, dammit!'

'How long have we gone now?' asked another student. 'We're going too damn' far north instead of east. If there is anything we wouldn't see it.'

'You didn't go far enough east,' said someone else. 'How long have we been going east?'

At 5.15 Taylor radioed Port Everglades: 'We will fly 270 degrees until we hit the beach or run out of gas.' This was good news. If Taylor held that course he would eventually reach the mainland.

Only fragmentary messages were received during the next forty-five minutes. The weather was deteriorating fast. Conditions were not bad at Fort Lauderdale, but over the Bahamas it was cloudy with poor visibility and Palm Beach was reporting foul conditions.

An unidentified voice from Flight 19 was heard shortly after six: 'What course are we on? We are over the Gulf . . . we didn't go far enough east. How long have we been on this course? I suggest we fly east until we run out of gas, we have a better chance of being picked up close to shore.

Taylor's voice: 'Holding course 270 degrees . . . we didn't go far enough east . . . turn around again . . . we may just as well turn around and go east again.'

Flight 19 changed course. Meanwhile, the Gulf and Frontier HF/DF nets had been completing a triangulation of bearings on Flight 19 and had managed to get a radio fix. The majority of sources on the Bermuda Triangle either fail to mention this or claim that only one fix was obtained and that a single fix is next to useless. In fact six different radio stations obtained several radio bearings and the completed triangulation located Flight 19 within a 100 miles radius of 29° 15' north, 79° 00' west – about 150 miles north of Fort Lauderdale, north of the Bahamas, and east of the Florida coast. This bearing was transmitted to several naval stations – but nobody thought to tell Flight 19!

At 6.20 a huge PBY flying boat took to the night sky from Dinner Key, a seaplane base at Miami. It set out to search for the five Avengers, but developed antenna trouble and was forced to return to base.

By this time Flight 19 was about thirty minutes from fuel exhaustion and Lt Taylor was heard to announce: 'All 'planes close up tight . . . we will have to ditch unless landfall . . . when the first 'plane drops to ten gallons we all go down together.' These were the last clear words received from Lt Taylor.

At 7.27 another PBY flying boat, BUNO 59225, left the Naval Air Station at Banana River with a crew of thirteen. In command was Lt Walter G. Jeffrey (not Harry G. Cone or Robert F. Cox, as is said in some sources). The huge aircraft sent a routine departure report just before 7.30. An hour later, when the 'plane did not send her hourly position report, the radioman at Banana River tried to establish contact. He was greeted by silence. The flying boat had vanished!

There was an intensive search operation, the largest of its kind at that time, but after five fruitless days it was called off because of a dramatic deterioration in the weather. No trace of the Lost Patrol was ever found. Not a shred of wreckage or debris, not even an oil slick. Six aircraft had totally vanished in the space of a few hours.

It is hardly surprising that the loss of six aircraft in such remarkable circumstances attracted worldwide interest, but the Bermuda Triangle legend has twisted the story to make it look even more mysterious. In reality it is not too difficult to understand what happened that afternoon.

To begin with, the loss of the seaplane was a separate incident from the disappearance of Flight 19 and her fate was known that night, long before anyone fully understood the factors which had combined to down the Lost Patrol. Most sources have the seaplane taking off between 4 o'clock and four-thirty; in fact the aircraft took off at seven-thirty, so the sources have it vanishing some three hours or more before it even left the runway. At 7.50 a tanker, SS *Gaines Mills*, was about 45 miles from Banana River when she observed a burst of flames. Her skipper later confirmed that he had seen an aircraft explode. The tanker stopped and circled a huge pool of oil, using searchlights to scan the water for wreckage. Debris littered a large area but the sea was too violent for it to be picked up. No bodies were seen. Confirmation that an aircraft had exploded came from the skipper of the USS *Solomons,* an aircraft carrier participating in the search for Flight 19. He reported that the carrier's air-search radar had tracked a 'plane leaving the Banana River Naval Air Station and proceeding on a course 045 degrees. The 'plane disappeared from the radar screen at the same time and in the same place as the *Gaines Mills* had seen an aircraft explode. There is no doubt that the aircraft tracked on the *Solomons'* radar was the seaplane, as must have been the explosion reported by the *Gaines Mills,* for it occurred exactly where the 'plane would have been after 23 minutes of flight.

Nobody knows what caused the seaplane to explode, but these aircraft were called 'flying gas-tanks' because they carried such a large quantity of high-octane fuel. In a sense they were flying bombs. Fumes from the fuel inside the hull could be lit by a spark; the crew were forbidden to carry anything that might ignite it, but a short circuit in a piece of equipment could have caused the disaster.

As for Flight 19, several factors are thought to have combined to cause the accident. Lt Taylor had never flown the route to be taken that day. For the past six months he had been stationed in Miami. Taylor was very familiar with the Florida Keys, but he did not know that from the air Great Sale Cay looks remarkably similar to the Keys. Seeing Great Sale Cay below, he thought that his students had flown off course and that Flight 19 was over the Keys, but he could not decide whether he was to the east of the Florida Peninsula and over the Gulf of Mexico or west of the Peninsula and over the Atlantic.

None of the Avengers had a clock and nobody had a watch. Taylor started flying in unknown directions for unknown lengths of time and became thoroughly confused. It began to grow dark and the weather deteriorated. Taylor was determined to keep the flight together and refused to change his radio frequency to the rescue channel. Flight 19 flew back and forth over the Bahamas until Taylor announced that all the aircraft would ditch when the first 'plane dropped to ten gallons of fuel. This moment eventually came and all five Avengers descended through the winter darkness towards the violent ocean below.

Several of the sources claim that Avenger aircraft have

been known to stay afloat for up to half an hour, plenty
of time in which to launch the life rafts and for the crew to
climb aboard – probably without even getting their feet wet,
one writer comments. In fact it must have been a memorable
day when an Avenger stayed afloat for thirty minutes; these
aircraft usually sink within twenty seconds to one minute,
so there isn't much time for a stunned crew to launch life
rafts.

Ditching, even in a calm sea, is a hazardous task for even
experienced pilots, and it is unlikely that four student pilots
could have successfully ditched at night and during a storm.
Even if there were survivors, which is unlikely, and they
did manage to evacuate the aircraft, it is improbable that
they would have survived for long in the prevailing seas.

Moreover, the search for Flight 19 did not begin until
after dusk, when the search craft stood next to no chance
of finding wreckage in the dark. Trying to spot debris from
a search aircraft at several hundred feet in the dark and
during bad weather is rather like trying to spot a contact
lens in a bath tub of water in a dark room from atop a step
ladder. By dawn the action of the sea would have dispersed
the wreckage over a vast area.

There cannot be any real doubt that this is what happened
to Flight 19, aptly called the Lost Patrol, but there are still
a few questions without answers. For example, why didn't
Lt Taylor want to fly that day? Lt Arthur A. Curtis,
Aviation Training Officer at Fort Lauderdale, told the
Board of Inquiry that Lt Taylor did not exhibit any unusual
behaviour and seemed normal in all respects. The Board
asked Lt Curtis six questions concerning Taylor's request to
be replaced and the matter was not raised again. It does not
appear that the investigators considered Lt Taylor's request
to have had any bearing on the disaster; in 1947 a page was
added to the report which absolved Taylor of all blame.
However, although it is unlikely that the Navy would not
have pursued the matter if they thought that Lt Taylor had
been unfit to take the flight out, it is not known why he
wanted another flight instructor to take his place. In view
of what happened one might be justified in wondering if
Taylor's judgement was in fact impaired.

At four o'clock Taylor told Cox that he had believed his

students to have taken a wrong turn on the second leg of the flight, but he added, 'I'm sure now that neither of my compasses are working.' Flight 19 had been given a thorough pre-flight check before take-off and everything was in perfect working order, yet both compasses in Lt Taylor's 'plane failed. How? Why? Is it possible that Taylor only *thought* that his compasses were out? When he saw Great Sale Cay below, did he assume that his instruments were wrong because he fully believed that the islands below were the familiar Florida Keys? Either way, at four o'clock, Taylor knew that he had made a mistake yet he persisted with the erroneous assumption that he was over the Keys. Why?

Contrary to several sources, Lt Taylor was not gripped by panic. He was a cool and courageous man who tried to keep his flight together, yet he refused to let a 'plane with a good compass take over the lead; refused to change radio frequencies to the rescue channel; and refused to listen to his students who had flown the area before and who seem to have known exactly where they were. Why Taylor behaved as he did is something which will forever remain unknown, but he was a brave man who, to quote the report, 'realised at an early hour that an emergency existed; that he promptly took charge, kept his flight together, and thereafter valiantly attempted to bring the flight home . . .'.

As I have said, the story of Flight 19 is the foundation upon which the 'mystery' of the Bermuda Triangle was built, yet many of those who have written about the region and claimed to have researched their information, tell and continue to tell of those spurious messages with which I opened this chapter. Where did those messages originate? The earliest source appears to be an article, 'The Mystery of the Lost Patrol' by Allan W. Eckert, which appeared in the April 1962 issue of *The American Legion Magazine*. Mr Eckert cannot now remember his source. In his book *The Bermuda Triangle* Charles Berlitz says that much of his information about Flight 19 came from the firsthand notes of Commander R. H. Wirshing, then a lieutenant on duty at Fort Lauderdale. In the BBC television documentary about the Bermuda Triangle Commander Wirshing denied having kept firsthand notes and said that he hadn't entered the

tower until after Flight 19 could no longer receive messages
from Fort Lauderdale. He said that he had not heard any
messages about the sea looking different or the pilots not
knowing which way was west. So the origin of those
messages is unknown, except that they didn't come from
the mouth of Lt Taylor.*

*In reply to an article of mine in *Pursuit*, the Journal of the Society for
the Investigation of the Unexplained, Charles Berlitz made two interesting
claims. He said that the BBC Television programme, *The Case of the
Bermuda Triangle*, was a good example of manipulative reporting in which
interviews were doctored so as to change the meaning of what was said.
He also says that Lawrence Kusche brought such pressure on Commander
Wirshing to change his story that Wirshing had to threaten legal action
before Kusche could be halted. The BBC deny that any item in the programme was doctored. As for threatened legal action against Kusche,
whether or not this is true does not alter Commander Wirshing's statements
to the BBC which were contrary to Berlitz's claims.

11 Three of Our Aircraft are Missing

The British General Election in the summer of 1945 resulted in a resounding and somewhat surprising victory for the Labour Party and on 26 July Clement Attlee became Prime Minister of the first majority Labour Government in British history. The new government soon embarked on a programme of nationalisation, the first step along the path towards fulfilling Labour's promise to restore security and prosperity to those gloomy post-war days. In 1946 the Civil Aviation Act nationalised British air transport. Privately owned airlines were either bought out or permitted only to operate charter flights, and were replaced by three state-owned corporations – British Overseas Airways Corporation (BOAC), British European Airways (BEA) and the British South American Airways Corporation (BSAAC).

In October 1946 an announcement from 10 Downing Street gave details of a government reshuffle. The Minister for Civil Aviation would now be Harry Louis Nathan (Lord Nathan of Churt), who would replace Lord Winster, who was to become Governor of Cyprus. Lord Nathan met the senior members of his staff one wet October morning. He told them, 'I don't know anything about civil aviation, but I have determined the policy of safety first, safety second and safety third.' It is accordingly ironic that two of the most baffling losses in the history of civil aviation should have occurred during the term of office of a man who held air safety in such high regard, and that a third disaster should have happened shortly after he retired from politics.

All three disasters happened to 'planes operated by British South American Airways, who had their offices in Grafton Street, Mayfair. It was here, in January 1946, that fifteen men used to meet in an upstairs room to discuss the operation of the new airline. In charge was the Corporation's

Chief Executive, Air Vice-Marshal Donald Clifford Tyndall Bennett. History will best remember Don Bennett as the creator and commanding officer of the Pathfinder Force, the RAF's élite of the élite who flew in advance of RAF bombers and identified enemy targets by dropping flares and large incendiaries.

The last word from the Star Dust

The first BSAAC aircraft to vanish was a Lancastrian Mk III airliner, G-AGWH *Star Dust*. Built in 1945 by A. V. Roe and Company of Manchester. England, she was delivered to BSAAC in early 1946 and from then until 22 July 1947 she was in constant use and clocked up a total of just over 1655 hours' flying time.

On 2 August 1947 a York aircraft belonging to BSAAC landed at Buenos Aires airport. Many of the passengers were bound for Santiago-de-Chile, a flight which involved crossing the Andes, and it was customary to transfer to a Lancastrian for the final leg of the flight. On this occasion passengers from the York transferred to the *Star Dust*.

The Captain was R. J. Cook DSO, DFC, DFM. He had served as a navigator with the RAF during the war and joined BSAAC in 1946. Now, at 29 years of age, he had made several trans-Andean crossings, but this was his first in command. His First Officer was N. H. Cook, also a former pilot with the RAF; he had never crossed the Andes before. D. S. Checklin was Second Officer. With the exception of the stewardess, he was the youngest member of the crew; he was nevertheless very experienced, having flown 2,074 hours with the RAF and BSAAC. The Radio Officer, D. B. Harmer, had served with the RAF as a wireless operator (Ground Duties) for three years before joining BSAAC in November 1946. The final member of the crew was Iris Moreen Evans, the stewardess or 'Star Girl'. She had served as a Chief Petty Officer in the WRNS before joining BSAAC in February 1947. The *Star Dust* also carried six passengers, a total of eleven people.

The trans-Andean flight to Santiago was arduous. The vast mountain system of the Andes is less than 100 miles wide, but extends for 4,500 miles from north to south, dividing South America into two distinct parts. The average height of the chain is about 13,000 feet, but several peaks rise as high as 20,000 feet, and one mountain, Aconcagua, in Argentina, near the Chile frontier, soars to 22,835 feet. BSAAC had planned three trans-Andean routes. The most direct route was to fly over the Andes 30 nautical miles* to the south of Mendoza. Alternatively, one could fly *via* San Juan, about 100 miles to the north of Mendoza, or south through the Planchon Pass. Bad weather made the central route hazardous and Commander Cook was warned in London and Buenos Aires against taking that route if the weather conditions were doubtful. In the event, the weather was poor and Commander Cook should have gone *via* San Juan or the Planchon Pass; instead he took the direct central route.

At 1.46pm (GMT) the *Star Dust* lifted from the runway at Buenos Aires and set course for Santiago. The flight was expected to take 3 hours 45 minutes and ETA was set at 5.31pm. The aircraft carried $6\frac{1}{2}$ hours of fuel, which left $2\frac{3}{4}$ hours' worth in the tanks to cope with any problems en route or upon arrival.

Over the next couple of hours the 'plane sent several position reports, each giving altitude as 10,000 feet. At 4.45, Santiago sent a weather report. It did not provide any information not already known to Captain Cook, but it emphasised an earlier report that cloud top was at 23,000 feet. The danger presented to aircraft by cloud is the risk of icing; ice can build up on an aircraft and result in a loss of power; but this only happens near freezing levels; above that altitude the water particles are frozen and do not stick to the aircraft. To avoid icing, Captain Cook should have flown above cloud top.

At 5.00pm, Captain Cook reported his height as 20,000 feet and ascending to 24,000 feet; 1,000 feet above cloud top.

At 5.30pm the *Star Dust* radioed ETA 5.45pm, just fifteen minutes away. During these fifteen minutes something happened, something which resulted in a radio message which has baffled accident investigators for over thirty years. At 5.41pm, only four minutes away from ETA, Mr Harmer, the Radio Operator, sent a single, mystifying word –

*One nautical mile = 6,080 feet; 1 statute mile = 5,280 feet.

'STENDEC'. The Chilean Air Force operator at Santiago later told accident investigators that the message was received loud and clear and given out very fast. He did not understand what the word meant and asked for it to be repeated. Twice in rapid succession the aircraft radioed 'STENDEC'.

Quarter of an hour passed without word from the *Star Dust* and every attempt to contact the aircraft was greeted by silence. A state of partial emergency was declared. One hour later a state of full emergency was announced and the search-and-rescue procedure was put into operation. Three aircraft from the Chilean Air Force Station at Colina undertook a preliminary search along the *Star Dust*'s track from Santiago as far as the entry of the El Christo Pass, but as darkness fell and the 'planes returned to base nothing had been found. The radio station at Santiago continued to call the *Star Dust* and all stations along the airliner's route maintained radio watch on the relevant frequencies for any message from the aircraft. The Amateur Radio Operators' Club of Chile was also provided with the *Star Dust*'s radio frequency and asked to be alert for the slightest hint of sound from the 'plane.

The next day a full-scale search was launched. The Chilean and Argentinian Air Force pressed aircraft into an organised search, and these were joined by more 'planes belonging to flying clubs and private owners. Meanwhile, ski-troops, skilled mountaineers and automobile parties formed groups and began patrolling an area of about 250 square miles. Nothing was found. The *Star Dust* and the eleven people on board had vanished into thin air!

The Accident Investigations Branch of the Ministry of Civil Aviation conducted an investigation. Their report, published in 1948, failed to reach any definite conclusions, although reference was made to Captain's Cook's choice of route:

As this was the pilot's first trans-Andean flight in command, and in view of the weather conditions, he should not have crossed by the direct route. Through lack of evidence due to no wreckage having been found the actual cause of the accident remains obscure. The possibility of severe icing cannot be ignored.

Was severe icing the cause of the disaster? The only place where icing could have occurred was in the El Christo Pass. The Pass was in cloud and it was snowing. A gale had started at midday and winds of 33 knots had steadily increased during the afternoon, gusts reaching a maximum of 62 knots. There would have been severe turbulance and icing could have occurred. However, the *Star Dust* was flying at 1,000 feet above cloud top, so, providing the cloud-top estimate was accurate, icing would not have occurred during this stage of the flight. In any event, the question of icing in the El Christo Pass is academic; when the *Star Dust* sent it last message it was four minutes away from Santiago, about 15 miles. Any accident due to icing in the El Christo Pass would have happened much earlier.

When the last message was received the *Star Dust* was at a low height, descending in preparation to land. She was not pressurised, so descent would have begun about half an hour earlier. The predominant cloud-type at Santiago was altocumulus, the type sometimes known as a 'mackerel sky', and it is unlikely to have caused any difficulties. With the exception of the El Christo Pass, it seems unlikely that the disaster was due to ice accretion, although, as the report states, the possibility cannot be ignored.

The Accident Report dealt only with facts and did not indulge in speculation; it therefore ignored one plausible theory: the crew was largely inexperienced on the route and possessed few navigational aids. It is possible that strong headwinds, particularly in the vicinity of the El Christo Pass, could have impeded forward progress yet gone unnoticed by the crew. This would mean that the *Star Dust* was further away from Santiago (perhaps even blown way off course) than the pilot believed. He would thus have begun descent earlier than otherwise would have been the case and may well have collided with high ground.

Whether this theory or any other is correct will have to wait until wreckage of the *Star Dust* is located. The rusting remains probably lie somewhere in the Andes Mountains about 40 miles east of Santiago. Wreckage thought to be of a Lancastrian was spotted in 1957, but investigation proved that it was the remains of an American aircraft that had disappeared in 1932!

The real mystery of the *Star Dust*, however, is that last message. In view of the fact that it was the last recorded message from the aircraft we must assume that it had some relevance and meant something to Mr Harmer, the Radio Operator, but accident investigators have been unable to come up with any theories. Thirty years later investigators cannot say more than what was said in the Accident Investigation Report: 'A solution to the word STENDEC has not been found.'

The Last Flight of the Star Tiger

In November 1947, just three months after the loss of the *Star Dust*, BSAAC accepted delivery of the *Star Tiger*. A little over two months later the aircraft left the tiny airport on Santa Maria in the Azores and vanished.

The *Star Tiger* disappeared in the Bermuda Triangle a little over two years after the famous 'Lost Patrol' (see pages 128 to 141 and it has accordingly received special attention in several books about the region. The last message from the 'plane, they say, was: 'Weather and performance excellent. Expect to arrive on schedule.' There was also a mysterious SOS, a faint distress call that was receding almost as if the *Star Tiger* were being dragged far away in space or time. And, most mysterious of all, a British Government investigation concluded its report with the words: 'some external cause must have overwhelmed both man and machine'; a comment which some people have interpreted as a veiled admission of inexplicable forces active in the Bermuda Triangle. In fact, *all* of this is incorrect.

In 1944 A. V. Roe began work on designs for a passenger aircraft based on the tried and trusted Lancaster bomber used so effectively by the RAF during the war. BOAC, who were looking for an aircraft for use on their London to New York route, became interested and submitted specifications. A. V. Roe produced an aircraft which they called the Tudor I; however, it did not fit all BOAC's requirements and was subject to certain defects (all of which were soon remedied), which resulted in BOAC rejecting the 'plane. There was a subsequent Government inquiry; the Courtnay Committee was appointed by the Ministry of Supply to investigate the rejection; but no decision had been reached by 1948 and the Tudor I had not gone into service. At this time, however, BSAAC were seeking a new airliner to replace their Lancastrian and York aircraft and, after considerable search around, had reached the conclusion that the Tudor I, with certain modifications, broadly suited their needs. A. V. Roe completed such alterations as were required and called the new model the Tudor IV.

The first Tudor IV, G-AHNJ *Star Panther*, flew in April 1947 and spent the next couple of months under inspection by officials of the Air Registration Board. It was issued with a Certificate of Airworthiness* in September and passed into service with BSAAC in October. Two more Tudor IVs were subsequently delivered to the airline, G-AHNK *Star Lion* and G-AHNP *Star Tiger*.

The *Star Tiger*, built at the Manchester factory of A. V. Roe, made her initial test flight on 4 November 1947 at Woodfield Aerodrome, Cheshire. She was given a Certificate of Airworthiness and delivered to BSAAC on 5 November. She left London Airport at eleven o'clock that night on her first scheduled flight to the West Indies. She returned on 12 November, and thereafter was in continuous use.

Before leaving on her last journey the *Star Tiger* was subject to a comprehensive maintenance check. The strict Maintenance Schedule required that all Tudor IVs should undergo such a check before or on completion of 600 flying hours. Since delivery to BSAAC the *Star Tiger* had made eleven journeys across the Atlantic, a total of 575 flying hours, and was accordingly given a thorough maintenance examination and a test flight before delivery to London Airport and her twelfth and last flight to Bermuda.

The Captain on that last flight was a New Zealander named Brian McMillan. He had come to Britain in 1937 to join the RAF as a pupil pilot. The first four years of the war were spent in India and Burma, where he won the Air

*A Certificate of Airworthiness is a document issued by the Air Registration Board which certifies that the design, construction and performance of a civil aircraft meet the specifications of the British Civil Airworthiness Requirements and is satisfactory in every respect as a flying machine. Such a certificate is issued after officials of the Air Registration Board have inspected the design, materials used, manufacturing process, and component parts, have conducted tests in the laboratory and in flight, and are satisfied that the high level of safety demanded by the Ministry of Civil Aviation is met.

Force Cross for his part in the evacuation during the retreat. In 1945 he joined the Pathfinder Force, earning the DSO and DFC. Following the end of the war, McMillan had joined Don Bennett – and others involved in this mystery – as one of the 'Grafton Street Fifteen', the founders of BSAAC. His ability as a pilot was unanimously praised by all who knew him and the report of the accident subsequently described him as a very steady and capable commander. He had clocked up 2,912 flying hours with the RAF and 1,673 with BSAAC.

There were five remaining members of the crew. The First Officer, a charming and friendly young man named David Colby, another former Pathfinder and again one of the 'Grafton Street Fifteen'. He had flown 1,690 hours with the RAF and 1,403 hours with BSAAC. This was to be his last flight as First Officer before taking command of his own Tudor IV. Cyril Ellison was the Second Officer and Navigator. Another former Pathfinder, he had flown 1,210 hours with the RAF, of which 1,050 had been as First Pilot. The Radio Officer was Robert Tuck, nicknamed Tucky. The oldest member of the crew, he had been a seagoing 'sparks' with the Merchant Navy for fourteen years and had spent the war as Senior Radio Officer at Prestwick with the RAF's Transatlantic Ferry Command. Since joining BSAAC he had flown 1,787 hours. As the only certified Wireless Telegraph Operator aboard he was responsible for all air-to-ground communications other than those made during take-off and landing or when the pilot specifically took over communication, Tucky was described as 'most experienced and capable'. Two 'Star Girls' completed the crew: Sheila Nichols and Lynn Clayton. Miss Clayton had been the brave survivor of a fatal air crash at Dakar nine months earlier.

Among the twenty-nine passengers were two VIPs. One was Air Marshall Sir Arthur Conningham, one of the outstanding air commanders of the war. He had recently retired from the RAF and was going to the Bahamas to spend a few days with an old friend. Sir Richard Fairey, head of the British aircraft manufacturing company of that name. The other VIP was H. Ernest Brooks, Assistant Secretary of the British Treasury, who, like Sir Arthur Conningham, was heading for the Bahamas.

On 27 January 1948 the *Star Tiger* left London Airport with a crew of six and twenty-three passengers. The flight to the West Indies was in three stages: from London to Lisbon, where an overnight stop was scheduled; then to Santa Maria in the Azores to take on fuel; and from there to Bermuda. During the flight to Lisbon the cabin heating (which had been noted as unreliable) and one of the compasses failed. The lack of heating made the flight uncomfortable and one of the passengers wrote in a letter that at 21,000 feet over the Bay of Biscay the temperature in the cabin was 34°F. It must have been with great relief that the passengers and crew disembarked at Lisbon for a hot dinner, some warmth and a night's rest.

The compass and the cabin heating apparatus were repaired during the night, but the next morning the port-inner engine failed. Take-off, scheduled for 9.15, was delayed for two hours while the fault was located. It turned out to be a failure of a priming pump and, in order to conduct the repair, it was necessary to turn off the petrol cocks to tanks three and four. The *Star Tiger* was powered by four liquid-cooled reciprocating engines manufactured by Rolls-Royce. These drew their fuel from a distributing tank connected by a pipeline to four flexible fuel tanks housed in the wings. On each pipeline there was a fuel cock. The cocks to tanks one and two were housed within the pilot's compartment, but three and four were located under the inboard engine nacelle and could be operated only when the 'plane was on the ground. This meant that if the cocks to tanks three and four were left in the 'off' position following the repairs to the port-inner engine, no fuel would have been drawn from those tanks and starvation would have occurred. Captain McMillan, being unable to turn the cocks on, would have had little chance of averting disaster. However, the Station Engineer at Lisbon later testified that he had definitely turned the cocks on after completing the repairs, and it is highly probable that this was the case. In any event it is unlikely that fuel starvation would have occurred, as we shall see.

The *Star Tiger*, with two additional passengers, bringing the total number of people on board to thirty-one, left Lisbon at 11.45am on the second leg of the flight to the Azores, a widely separated group of islands about 900 miles to the west of Lisbon. The heating apparatus and the troublesome compass failed again soon after take-off.

During the war the British had constructed a small runway on Santa Maria, the easternmost island of the Azores, and it was here, in the middle of the afternoon of Wednesday, 28 January, that Brian McMillan brought the *Star Tiger* in to land against a 60-knot headwind. The 'plane came to a halt in less than 200 yards.

The third stage of the flight was the most arduous and, although Santa Maria was scheduled as a refuelling stop of $1\frac{1}{2}$ hours, it was customary to check the weather conditions for the rest of the flight before proceeding. McMillan accordingly went to the Meteorological Office, where he was warned of adverse conditions ahead; he decided to stop at Santa Maria overnight. He was not the only pilot to have made such a decision. Frank Griffin, another former Pathfinder and one of the 'Grafton Street Fifteen', had also decided to stop for the night. He was piloting a BSAAC Lancastrian with a cargo of freight to Bermuda, where the freight was to be transferred to the *Star Tiger*. He could probably have reached Bermuda, the Lancastrian having long-range tanks and an endurance of 19 hours, but he saw no reason to risk a journey in poor weather only to arrive a day ahead of the Tudor IV.

The passengers disembarked for an unexpected overnight stay and after dinner they joined the crew in the small bar of the airport hotel. McMillan went to bed about 9.00pm saying that he was very tired, leaving Griffin talking to an RAF friend, Anthony J. Mulligan, who was bound for Bermuda with his wife and father.

The next morning, 29 January, McMillan, Colby and Griffin went to the Meteorological Office to obtain a flight forecast. There was a slight improvement, but a strong headwind opposed flights to Bermuda. The captains calculated flight plans for various heights, but decided that because the winds increased in strength with height it would be best to proceed at 2,000 feet. It was rare – and still is – for long-distance flights to be conducted so low, the danger lying in the fact that the lower the altitude the less time allowed in which to cope with an emergency. Accident investigators later agreed that there was no reason to regard 2,000 feet as unsafe providing the crew maintained normal vigilance.

It was decided that Griffin would leave one hour ahead of the *Star Tiger*. The Lancastrian's long-range tanks and high endurance allowed it to cope more easily with any adverse conditions than could the *Star Tiger*, and Griffin would be able to radio news of any problems back to McMillan. The Lancaster left Santa Maria at 2.22 GMT (12.22 Azores time and 10.22 in Bermuda); the flight was expected to take 12 hours 28 minutes.

Meanwhile, Captain McMillan had a problem. The Traffic Assistant at the Azores had prepared a load sheet and found that the all-up weight of the *Star Tiger* exceeded the maximum weight permitted by the Certificate of Airworthiness. McMillan had a choice: leave some passengers behind or reduce his fuel load by 150 gallons. He was naturally reluctant to do either, but told the Traffic Assistant that he would reduce the fuel load. However, when the engineer came to fill up the tanks, McMillan told him: 'Fill her up to the gills.' The *Star Tiger* therefore left Santa Maria with an excess weight of 936 pounds. This overload reduced the safety of the flight only during take-off and the early stages. The report of the Court investigation states:

> This overload was soon reduced by fuel consumption and cannot of course have had anything to do with the disaster. Captain McMillan's insistence on full tanks does, however, indicate that he fully appreciated the difficulties occasioned by the prevalent headwinds.

The 'prevalent headwinds' mentioned in the report composed the most dangerous feature of the route from the Azores to Bermuda. The shortest route from Santa Maria to Bermuda lies across 1,961 nautical miles of featureless ocean. The fuel capacity of the Tudor IV was sufficient for it to reach Bermuda, but not to proceed beyond, the nearest land being the wreck-strewn coast of Cape Hatteras some 580 miles away, well beyond the Tudor's endurance.

Unfortunately, Bermuda is prone to sudden and unexpected tropical storms which make landing difficult and dangerous.

Such storms are infrequent and rarely last for more than two hours, but their sudden appearance can take approaching aircraft by surprise. BSAAC therefore demanded that aircraft should arrive with at least two hours' fuel in the tanks, sufficient to cope with any unforeseen problems. This safety margin was not always possible, however, particularly during winter, when aircraft flying from the Azores encountered headwinds.

BSAAC, fully aware of the dangers presented by their trans-Atlantic route, took every possible precaution to ensure flight safety. The flight was divided into three phases, each phase being determined by the Captain before leaving the Azores and based on prevailing winds, the height and weight at which the 'plane was flying, and the quantity of fuel carried:

Phase One: During the first stage the 'plane has sufficient fuel to return to Santa Maria if conditions became hazardous.

Phase Two: The Point of No Return. Beyond this point the haven of Santa Maria slips out of reach and the 'plane is committed to onward flight. However, there remains sufficient fuel to reach an alternative airport in Newfoundland.

Phase Three: The Point of No Alternative. The aircraft now enters the most critical stage in the flight. Newfoundland is now beyond reach and the aircraft must head for and land at Bermuda or go down in the sea.

Further precautions required BSAAC pilots to transmit an 'all's well' message every thirty minutes and to send a position report every hour to Oceanic Air Traffic Control (OATC), which is responsible for the safety of aircraft until the aircraft is approaching an airport, when control is taken over by Airport Approach Control, and when the aircraft is overhead, when control is handled by Airfield Approach Control.

During the first half of the flight the *Star Tiger* would be under the control of OATC Station CSY, Azores. For the remainder of the journey control would be handled by OATC Station WSY, New York, either communicating direct or through Station VRT, Bermuda, an Air Guard service provided on behalf of OATC New York by Cable and Wireless (West Indies) Ltd. Station VRT Bermuda was required to hear from any aircraft under its control every thirty minutes. The written orders demanded that a state of emergency be declared if no word was heard from the 'plane and if the VRT operator failed to establish contact. If further attempts to raise the aircraft failed, a state of distress emergency had to be declared and all rescue services alerted.

The *Star Tiger* left Santa Maria at 3.34pm on 29 January, climbed to 2,000 feet and set course for the long and arduous flight to Bermuda. With full fuel tanks the Tudor's endurance was 16 hours and McMillan estimated that the flight would take just under $12\frac{1}{2}$ hours, placing ETA about four o'clock the following morning. The fuel reserve would be $3\frac{1}{2}$ hours, a reserve which would be more than enough to cope with any problems.

The weather was as forecast: at 2,000 feet an impene-trable bank of stratocumulus reached down in patches of squall to the grey, wind-whipped ocean below. There was severe turbulence and the passengers may have felt a little queasy. Few would be that time have relished the thought of the evening meal being prepared at the rear of the cabin by the Star Girls, but this stage of the journey promised to be the most comfortable in that the cabin heating apparatus was unnecessary at the low height of 2,000 feet.

The crew was variously occupied. Of importance in regard to subsequent events is Cyril Ellison, the Navigator. He had three methods of navigation:

Dead Reckoning: Calculating the aircraft's position by estimating the wind velocity and the direction, speed and course of the aircraft. It is not the most satisfactory method of navigation since the calculated position would be in error if any of the estimated factors were different from the actual.

Astronavigation: Navigation by observation of the stars with a sextant. The Azores–Bermuda route was planned so that the greater part of the journey could be made during the hours of darkness. In good conditions a star-fix taken by an experienced navigator like Cyril Ellison would mean an error in navigation of not more than fifteen miles.

Radio Bearings: A continuous signal transmitted by the radio operator to a ground station where a directional aerial system ascertains the aircraft's position and the information is sent to the aircraft.

Ellison's first position report at shortly before 4.00pm was computed by dead reckoning, the first of many such to come.

Shortly after four o'clock McMillan called Tucky on the intercom and asked him to contact the Lancastrian and see what weather Griffin was experiencing. Some ten minutes later the first inter-aircraft communication took place. Nothing adverse was reported.

At 4.52pm Griffin radioed New York *via* OATC Azores requesting a landing forecast for Bermuda between 3am and 4am the next day and for a wind forecast for the later stages of the flight.

At five o'clock Ellison gave Tucky the second position report, another computed by dead reckoning.

Griffin was still awaiting a reply to his request and after inquiries learned that New York had not received his message. He repeated it. Forty-five minutes later he still hadn't heard from New York and in desperation told his radio officer to contact the United States Army Air Force base at Kindley Field, Bermuda: 'Landing forecast and upper winds urgently required.'

Six o'clock came and went. Tucky transmitted Ellison's third position report, another computed by dead reckoning. At 6.05pm the US Army Air Force replied to Griffin's request. It was not good news; winds along the Lancastrian's route were stronger than forecast by Santa Maria. Griffin's nevigator confirmed this and also made an alarming discovery. According to his calculations the winds presently experienced by the Lancastrian were 55 knots as against the 30 to 40 knots forecast by Santa Maria. On the basis of this new information, Griffin decided to advance his flight time by one hour from 12.28 to 13.28. At 6.49 he radioed Santa Maria with a message for the *Star Tiger*: 'My flight time now on revised winds, 13.28. What do you think?' McMillan agreed and amended his own flight time, advancing ETA from 3.56am to 5.00am. In fact, McMillan's calculation was inaccurate. At the *Star Tiger*'s position and speed and in light of the new wind forecast, ETA should have been 5.30am. This delay was more serious for the *Star Tiger* than for the Lancastrian, but it cannot be said to be disturbing. The *Star Tiger*'s safety margin for dealing with a further deterioration in the weather or with unforeseen problems at Bermuda was reduced to two hours, but was still within the prescribed limits.

At seven o'clock Tucky transmitted Ellison's fourth position report, another calculated by dead reckoning.

At 7.30pm New York established direct contact with the Lancastrian and informed Griffin that a message was on the way from Bermuda. He was told to stand by. Griffin stood by but there was no message. Having wasted time waiting, it was not until 7.45pm that he contacted the *Star Tiger* and passed on the weather information sent to him by the US Air Force base some $1\frac{3}{4}$ hours earlier. However, as Tucky was working on the same frequency as Griffin, it is probable that he overheard the broadcast.

At eight o'clock Tucky transmitted another dead-reckoning position report. The *Star Tiger* had been airborne for four hours thirty minutes. Two hours ahead lay the Point of No Return. ETA was still $9\frac{1}{2}$ hours distant. The halfway stage in the flight was now less than forty-five minutes away.

At 8.43pm VRT Bermuda established direct communication with both aircraft and passed a wind-and-landing forecast. A few minutes later the *Star Tiger* reached the half-way stage in her flight and VRT Bermuda accepted Air Guard responsibilities.

At 9.00pm Tucky transmitted the sixth successive position report computed by dead reckoning. The Point of No Return was now only one hour away.

Shortly before ten o'clock a patch in the overcast gave Cyril Ellison the chance to take a star shot and the position report was thus the first to be calculated by astronavigation. The *Star Tiger* had now completed the first phase of the flight. Increased headwinds had reduced the fuel margin, but McMillan's reserve was still within the prescribed limits and the flight had otherwise been uneventful. The *Star Tiger* passed the Point of No Return and the Azores slipped beyond reach.

No word was heard from the *Star Tiger* for the next fifty-five minutes until Tucky sent Ellison's eleven o'clock position report, another computed by dead reckoning. Tucky should have radioed an 'all's well' signal at ten-thirty, but it doesn't appear to have been sent. Moreover, Mr Richards, the VRT Bermuda operator, should have attempted to raise the aircraft after a silence of thirty minutes and, in the event that he failed, to declare a state of emergency. In not doing so he had not complied with his orders.

Shortly after eleven o'clock a power failure at Bermuda prevented teleprinter communication between VRT and BSAAC's offices. The telephone was unaffected and Mr Richards told the Court of Inquiry into the loss of the *Star Tiger* that he had attempted to pass the report by telephone but had been unable to get a reply. The BSAAC Station Manager, Wing-Commander Ralph, could not explain why the telephone had not been answered. His office was continually manned, he said.

A few minutes before midnight Tucky transmitted Ellison's position report, again computed by dead reckoning. This was the first word heard from the *Star Tiger* for forty-two minutes, the second time that a period of thirty minutes had been allowed to elapse without VRT attempting to make contact.

By midnight the power failure had been rectified. The *Star Tiger* was now 750 miles from Bermuda and only $1\frac{1}{2}$ hours from the Point of No Alternative.

Shortly before one o'clock Ellison managed to get a star shot, but nothing disturbing was revealed. The Point of No Alternative was half an hour away.

At 1.26am Mr Bunker, Frank Griffin's navigator, 150 miles ahead of the *Star Tiger*, managed to get his first star shot in several hours and made an alarming discovery. The winds in the Lancastrian's present position had been forecast by Santa Maria as 'light and variable', but according to his calculations the Lancastrian was experiencing a south-westerly wind of some 48 knots and had been blown about 68 miles off course during the preceding hour!

Meanwhile, aboard *Star Tiger* nothing alarming had come to notice and at one thirty the aircraft passed the Point of No Alternative. *Star Tiger* was now committed to onward flight and to reaching Bermuda, a pin-head of land in a vast expanse of water.

At two o'clock a patch in the overcast gave Ellison the chance of another star shot and he learned that the *Star Tiger*, like the Lancastrian (although he was unaware of Mr Bunker's discovery), had been blown off course and in the direction of New York, a destination which could never have been reached. Ellison computed a new course and McMillan unknowingly turned the *Star Tiger* into the teeth of a gale!

About this time Frank Griffin radioed VRT Bermuda for wind and weather information and was told: 'Wait.' Griffin waited for quarter of an hour and at 2.15, when nothing had been received, he repeated his request. There was no reply. He tried for a third time at 2.33 and again failed to get an answer. It was not until 2.42 that the VRT radioed: 'Winds SSW 20 knots.'

SSW 20 knots! That was half the force calculated by Mr Bunker and, while it is true that wind calculations deduced from position observations during flight are inexact, could Mr Bunker have miscalculated the wind velocity to this extent?

It was now almost three o'clock. Tucky transmitted the position report, dead reckoning again, and a few minutes later Frank Griffin radioed McMillan. He was about an hour out of Bermuda: 'Changing now to voice telephony to contact Bermuda Approach Control,' he said, and added: 'See you at breakfast.' Griffin landed safely at 4.11am (12.11am Bermuda Time).

After communication with Griffin, McMillan asked Tucky to get a radio bearing from Bermuda. As stated, a radio bearing is obtained by the radio operator keeping the transmitting key depressed and sending a continuous signal to the ground station which, with the aid of a directional aerial system, plots the aircraft's position and sends the information to the aircraft. On this occasion, however, a satisfactory bearing could not be obtained and the *Star Tiger* was asked to try again in fifteen minutes.

At 3.15am, when the *Star Tiger* was 340 nautical miles from Bermuda, Tucky repeated his request for a radio bearing. Two minutes later VRT sent a First Class Bearing of 72 degrees. The *Star Tiger* acknowledged receipt.

This was really good news. A First Class Bearing was unlikely to be in error by more than two degrees and McMillan no doubt felt more relaxed than he had done for some time. The *Star Tiger* was on course and a series of radio bearings would guide her safely into Bermuda.

The minutes ticked by without word from the *Star Tiger*. At 3.50am, after a silence of thirty-five minutes, Mr Richards at VRT tried to raise the aircraft, but there was no reply. He contacted Bermuda Approach Control, thinking that the airliner might have changed radio frequencies to direct telephony for the approach to the islands, but Approach Control had no news. Ten minutes later Mr Richards again tried to raise the *Star Tiger* – still silence.

At 4.40am, ninety-five minutes since he'd last heard from the airliner and less than an hour from her ETA, Mr Richards made a final attempt to contact the 'plane. There was still no reply and Mr Richards declared a state of emergency. Within five minutes the Search and Rescue Section of the United States Army Air Force at Kindley Field, Bermuda, was alerted and the air-sea rescue arrangements were put into operation, direction of the search being assigned to the base commander, Colonel Thomas D. Ferguson.

The *Star Tiger*'s ETA came and went. Many radio operators had been listening on the relevant frequency but not a murmur had been heard from the aircraft.

At 7.16am (3.16am Bermuda time) the first search craft, a Fortress equipped with a radar scanner, left Kindley Field. Four hours had now passed since the last message from the *Star Tiger* had been received at 3.15am, ninety minutes had passed since ETA, and the aircraft, if it was still aloft, was only minutes away from fuel exhaustion.

News that the *Star Tiger* was overdue reached the American PX, where Griffin was having breakfast, and upon making a few inquiries Griffin learned that Geoffrey Rees (another Pathfinder and member of the 'Grafton Street Fifteen'), who was waiting with a relief crew to take the *Star Tiger* on to Jamaica, was planning to take out the Lancastrian and fly parallel to USAAF's Fortress' search. Although he had had no sleep for nearly twenty-four hours, Griffin joined Rees aboard the Lancastrian and they began to comb an area 300 to 400 miles northeast of Bermuda.

It was not until just after dawn that the search operation really got under way. Two B-25 bombers and a C-47 transport left Mitchell Field, New York, to search five hundred miles of Atlantic north from Ocean City, New Jersey, to Long Island. The Coastguard launched three PBY flying boats and the cutters *Mendota, Cherokee* and *Androscoggin.* Fourteen aircraft were added to the search by Air Transport Command (ATC), who also placed more aircraft on standby to join the hunt if the *Star Tiger* was not found within the next few hours. An ATC Transport and a B-17, both of which had landed at Bermuda, were returned to the sky, and six Pan-American World Airways airliners were diverted from their New York–Puerto Rico route to fly over the search area. Aircraft from as far afield as Stephensville, Newfoundland, Borninguen AFB, Puerto Rico, joined an enormous search which would last for five days.

On the first day the search was called off at dusk. Fifteen hours of tireless efforts had produced no material results and the weather was deteriorating. Colonel Ferguson was forced to ground all aircraft, and announced that the search would be resumed only if the weather improved. Referring to the wind-lashed ocean, he said: 'I doubt anyone could survive in seas like that.'

The weather grew worse overnight but the search resumed the next day, Saturday. During the day there were several reports. Captain W. M. Hackett, the pilot of a search 'plane combing an area 75-100 miles northeast of Bermuda, reported patches of oil. The area was thoroughly searched, but nothing was found. Captain Hackett's description of the oil slicks conformed with their being the type which result from bilge pumping, and it was later decided that they must have been made by a passing steamer.

A hopeful report came from two Pan-Am airliners which reported flares and a raft to the south of Bermuda. The tanker *Esso Philadelphia*, which was in the area, conducted a search and found a raft, but it was from a surface vessel and had been in the water for a very long time. The flares were never confirmed.

Dusk descended on Saturday, 31 January, without a scrap of debris from the *Star Tiger* having been found and, as the weather grew worse, so hope of finding survivors dwindled.

On Sunday a storm swept Bermuda, but seven aircraft nevertheless made sorties and hopes were raised when the pilot of a B-17 out of Westover Field, Massachusetts, sighted several yellow and black boxes and a cylindrical object that looked like an oil drum floating in the sea about 325 miles northeast of Bermuda. The Coast Guard sent the *Cherokee* and *Androscoggin* and the tug *Acunshet* to search the area, but no trace of the coloured boxes was found. However, a roll of sheet cork was located and is thought to have been the cylindrical object: it did not come from the *Star Tiger*.

The search for the *Star Tiger* had been called off on 3 February. Altogether, 104 flights had been undertaken and a total of 882 flying hours had been flown, most of them during extremely bad weather. Surface craft had also been employed and a continuous radio watch maintained. Late on Wednesday, 4 February, hope was revived for a short while when radio operators received an SOS signal. It was in code, although sent by somebody ignorant of Morse; the sender had laboriously tapped out one dot for 'A', two dots for 'B', and so on throughout the alphabet, spelling: S-T-A-R-T-I-G-E-R. A continuous watch was kept but the message was not repeated.

The message had been transmitted on an international frequency for voice communication, yet had been tapped out with a transmitting key, which was strange; the small radio transmitters in the *Star Tiger*'s rubber dinghies were for voice communication only and it was impossible for the airliner's heavy radio equipment to have been transferred to one of the dinghies. Nor was it possible that the *Star Tiger* was still afloat. Thus the only satisfactory explanation was that the message had been sent by a hoaxer.

The search for *Star Tiger* was not resumed. The report of the Court inquiry into the loss states:

It is only fitting that the Court should here record its admiration of the zeal and courage with which it [the search] was conducted; it is impossible to exaggerate the service rendered by the United States authorities and by all who contributed and managed the aircraft and vessels employed. The tragedy of the loss of the *Star Tiger* is rendered the more poignant by the fact that all their efforts were in vain. No trace of the aeroplane was found and no trace of wreckage or of any other object connected with her has since been seen.

The political storm surrounding the disappearance of the *Star Tiger* was still raging when, towards the end of February 1948, the certified accounts of the three state-owned airways for the financial year ending 31 March 1947 were published. BOAC and BEA had together made losses amounting to £10 million. Only BSAAC showed a profit, albeit only a small one, of £32,000. The public was outraged at this far from auspicious beginning to the nationalised airlines' first operational year. BSAAC's small profit kept them from the forefront of the tax-payers' wrath, but the loss of the *Star Tiger*, which illuminated the Corporation's many problems and brought to light several near disasters, made people wonder if BSAAC's profit was made at the expense of air safety.

In reality, BSAAC's profit was not a profit in the true sense of the word at all. The Corporation was able to charter aircraft from the government at exceptionally low rates, which in effect amounted to a hidden subsidy. As for the fact that there were no weather-ships along the route, this was the responsibility of the Ministry and had nothing to do with BSAAC.

On Monday, 22 March 1948 the Minister of Civil Aviation announced that the Court of Inquiry would be opened at 10.30am on 12 April at the Hoare Memorial Hall, Church House, Westminster, with Lord Hugh Pattison Baron Macmillan presiding.

The proceedings began as planned on 12 April and Mr Follick, the Labour MP for Loughborough, who had made much of the issue in Parliament, was one of the first witnesses. He told the Court that he had flown to the West Indies aboard the *Star Tiger* on 27 December. When 1½ hours from London the aircraft had had to turn back because of engine trouble, he said. At Lisbon there had been further problems and at Santa Maria the flight had been delayed because of bad weather. In the opinion of the passengers, he claimed, the *Star Tiger* was not in a fit state to undertake such an arduous journey. Geoffrey Rees, the pilot on that flight, and in his testimony denied that the *Star Tiger* was unsafe.

Air Vice-Marshal Donald Bennett admitted that BSAAC had suffered more accidents and near accidents than BOAC, but he denied that economy was the corporation's first consideration. 'We happen to have the misfortune, or probably good fortune as far as Britain was concerned, of creating an entirely new service in a new area,' he said. The loss of the *Star Tiger* was an inexplicable occurrence and he found it difficult to imagine any circumstances which could have brought such rapid disaster upon the aircraft. Although nothing could be excluded, he felt sure that the accident had not been due to any error on the part of the crew. When asked if he had a preferred opinion as to the cause of the accident, Bennett said: 'My own feeling in view of subsequent re-examinations is that the likelihood of accident through any of the wild suppositions of a flying nature is much less likely than sabotage.'

The Court considered every possible theory for the accident and the inquiry ended on 14 May. 'There could certainly not have been a more baffling problem for any tribunal to consider,' said Lord Macmillan.

In August 1948 the forty-nine page report was presented to the Minister of Civil Aviation and it was published as a White Paper on Tuesday, 28 September. The Court had considered every probable cause of the accident but failed to reach a conclusion:

There are no grounds for supposing that in the design of the Tudor IV aeroplane, or in the manufacture of the particular Tudor IV aeroplane *Star Tiger*, there were technical errors or omissions of a kind which offends against the highest accepted standards of good practice.

Nor are there any grounds for supposing that the loss of the *Star Tiger* was caused by any metereological hazard. The occurrence of a disastrous mechanical disruption of any part of the power plant cannot be ruled out on the evidence, but again the possibility is most remote.

The possibility of fire must be considered. It cannot be shown with certainty on the evidence that it did not occur

in this case, but it is nevertheless most improbable . . .
Every precaution is taken in the design to prevent it, and
this type of aircraft is well supplied with fire extinguishing
devices . . . had any serious fire occurred which was not
immediately controlled by the extinguishers, it is unlikely
that a distress message could not have been sent before
a catastrophe resulted . . . There is a possibility that a fire
occurred as a separate event after radio failure; this
requires the coincidence of two improbabilities.

And so the report continues, examining every possibility
and concluding that they were all too unlikely to have
occurred.

Considerable consideration was given to the possibility of
engine failure, but a mechanical failure of the engines was
discounted. The *Star Tiger* could fly safely on three engines;
indeed, at her weight at the relevant time, on two. 'The
possibility of simultaneous failure of two or more engines
due to mechanical causes is so remote as to be almost inconceivable, having in mind the long record of high reliability
possessed by engines of this general type,' says the report.

Engine failure due to fuel starvation could not be
eliminated, however. It was common practice when conduct-
ing long-range flights to turn off some tanks so that a known
quantity of fuel was retained for future use. This was not
usually done on Tudor IV aircraft and it was not Captain
McMillan's usual practice to do so, but, says the report, 'it
appears probable that if one or both of the cocks controlling
the No 1 tank had been turned off throughout the flight, one
pair of engines would have been starved of fuel during the
half hour following the last signal from the aircraft'. The
result of fuel starvation would have been a loss of power on
one side of the aircraft and the only indication of this would
have been a yawing motion as the constant-speed propellers
adjusted themselves to maintain the engine revolutions; there
would have been no obvious change in the noise or of the
instrument readings, but if immediate action were not taken
the *Star Tiger* would have gone into a dive, dropping 2,000
feet in fifteen seconds. Unless McMillan and Colby were very
alert it is unlikely that anything could have been done to
avert disaster – and both men had been flying for twelve

hours, so how alert would they have been? Alternatively, if the automatic pilot were engaged, the *Star Tiger* would have gone into a gentle spiral, losing about 1,000 feet a minute, so again there would have been very little time in which to take action.

While fuel starvation cannot be eliminated it is nonetheless unlikely. The radio operator was required to state the amount of fuel remaining in the tanks in his hourly position reports to OATC. At three o'clock Tucky had quoted the figure of 944 gallons. The 'plane probably had more than this; tests conducted on other Tudor IVs showed that, although the tanks were rated at 3,300 gallons, they could accommodate about another 100 gallons. Moreover, fuel consumption was calculated by referring to both the flowmeters and the tank-depth gauges, and these frequently gave different readings, so it was customary to quote the larger figure. McMillan would have noticed that the depth gauges for tank No 1 remained in the 'full' position when he came to calculate Tucky's report and, although he may at first have thought that there was a fault in the gauge, it would have become apparent that something was wrong when, as the flight progressed, the instruments showed an abnormally heavy drain on the other tanks. Finally, in the unlikely event of fuel starvation, the experts were certain that disaster would have overcome the *Star Tiger* long before 3.15am.

In its search for the cause of the accident the court gave careful consideration to the most likely mechanical and human failures and dismissed them as improbable, yet there is one indisputable fact – whatever happened to the *Star Tiger* and however suddenly it happened, Robert Tuck did not send a distress message. Why not?

The obvious explanation is radio failure, and there is no doubt that at this stage in the flight this would have created a critical situation affording little or no margin for error. In the circumstances McMillan's best hope of reaching Bermuda was with the aid of a series of radio bearings.

The *Star Tiger* carried two identical wireless-telegraphy transmitters, each with a range of several thousand miles, and three wireless telephony transmitter-receivers which had a range of about two hundred miles. All were powered by a DC electrical power supply of twenty-four volts provided by two six-kilowatt generators. Accumulators with a storage capacity of eighty ampere hours at twenty-four volts were also provided. Total radio failure would have required the simultaneous failure of both generators and the storage battery, and, in the words of the Court: 'It is very difficult to visualise a situation in which electrical failure would be likely to effect the battery and both generators.'

A further possibility is that Tucky was taken sick or otherwise unable to operate the wireless-telegraphy transmitter. He was the only qualified radio operator aboard the *Star Tiger* – except, perhaps, one of the passengers – and it is very likely that nobody else had the skill to operate the equipment. However, the radio telephony sets could have been operated by any member of the crew and, although they have less range than the telegraphy equipment, the *Star Tiger* would have been within range of Bermuda shortly after 3.15am and there is very little doubt that communication would have been possible.

Power failure, although unlikely, remains the most probable explanation for the lack of a distress call, yet it would not have upset the stability of the aircraft and on its own would not have brought about the disaster. However, it would have created a critical situation. Without radio bearings Cyril Ellison would have been faced with the task of plotting the *Star Tiger*'s course with nothing more than the data he already possessed. Besides knocking out the radio, power failure would have put the gyroscopic compass out of action too, leaving the 'plane with nothing but the two bowl compasses. The court report says that bowl compasses are highly accurate, but this is a very questionable statement because they are known to be subject to several types of error. Moreover, the flight from London to Santa Maria had been dogged by the continual failure of one of the compasses. The report does not say whether the offending piece of equipment was replaced at Santa Maria or merely repaired there. If the latter, it was likely to fail again. However, Ellison knew that the wind force was not as had been forecast. He also knew that the *Star Tiger* was taking a fairly large northerly drift rather than the forecast southerly drift and had compensated for this. He also had a radio bearing which is unlikely to have been in error by more than two degrees. Proceeding on this information Ellison could have plotted a course which should have brought him to within thirty miles of Bermuda by 5.30am, at which position he should have been able to see the powerful marine lights around the coast. Even in the unlikely event of complete power failure the *Star Tiger*, in the opinion of the court, should have been able to reach Bermuda – but was the court being overly optimistic?

At 3.15am, when the last message was received from the *Star Tiger*, the weather was rapidly deteriorating and the aircraft's reserve fuel had been reduced by headwinds stronger than forecast. Bermuda was a tiny dot of land some 340 miles and $2\frac{1}{2}$ hours flying time distant. If McMillan flew or was blown off course it is possible that he would not have seen the marine lights around the island and would have had just over an hour in which to find his destination before fuel exhaustion. If he failed he would have been forced to ditch. The sea was growing boisterous and the chance of successfully ditching a large airliner on rough seas and on a dark and overcast night are far from good. Even assuming that McMillan succeeded, there would have been precious little time in which to get thirty-one panic-stricken people into the dinghies before the aircraft sank. By the time a state of emergency was declared by VRT the *Star Tiger* could have been down for as long as ninety-five minutes, and a further two-and-a-half hours would elapse before the first search 'plane took off. The *Star Tiger* could have been down for maybe as long as eight or nine hours before the air-sea search really got underway. By this time any wreckage would have been dispersed by the sea. As for the survivors, they may have been drowned when their dinghy was capsized by a wave or maybe they drifted away from the scene of the accident and beyond the search area.

Nobody knows what really happened to the *Star Tiger*, but the story of her disappearance as it is told in many of the books on the Bermuda Triangle is patently inaccurate. The 'plane's last message was not 'Weather and performance excellent. Expect to arrive on schedule'; the weather was far from excellent and the aircraft did not expect to arrive on schedule because there were increased headwinds to prevent it from doing so. As for the court's statement that 'some external cause must have overwhelmed both man and machine', which is seen by some as a veiled reference to the supernatural forces alleged to exist in the Triangle, this was no more than a reference to anything other than human error or mechanical failure; i.e., the weather. Such is clear when the comment is put into context:

Into all activities which involve the co-operation of man and machine two elements enter of very diverse character. There is the incalculable element of the human equation dependent upon imperfectly known factors; and there is the mechanical element subject to quite different laws. A breakdown may occur in either separately or in both in conjunction. Or some external cause may overwhelm both man and machine.

The court considered many possible causes and failed to reach a satisfactory solution; nevertheless, it did not dismiss these causes as impossible: 'Some misfortune overtook this aircraft. It may have been one of those discussed in the preceding paragraphs, or a combination of them. Or it may have been an event of a kind which has not been considered here.'

And so the report came to an end: In closing this report it may truly be said that no more baffling problem has ever been presented for investigation . . . What happened in this case will never be known and the fate of the *Star Tiger* must remain an unsolved mystery.'

And an unsolved mystery it has remained.

Another of our aircraft is missing
On 17 January 1949, only thirteen days short of a year since the disappearance of the *Star Tiger*, the BSAAC airliner *Star Ariel* lifted from the runway at Kindley Field, Bermuda, and set course for Jamaica. A few hours later stunned officials of BSAAC announced that the aircraft had disappeared.

The *Star Ariel* was a Tudor IVB, similar to the Tudor IV but modified to incorporate accommodation for a Flight Engineer and an engineer's panel. She was delivered to BSAAC on 14 November 1948, and from that day had been in constant use, making three return flights from London to Havana. A fourth crossing had been cancelled at Lisbon because of undercarriage trouble.

On 13 January 1948 G-AGRE *Star Ariel* left London on her fifth scheduled flight to the West Indies. She reached Jamaica after a trouble-free and uneventful flight, and on 16 January she embarked on the return flight to London, stopping at Nassau in the Bahamas and Kindley Field, Bermuda, where she arrived at 9.32am, meeting another BSAAC airliner, the *Star Lion*, a sister aircraft of the *Star Tiger* and one of the first Tudors delivered to BSAAC.

The *Star Lion* had left London on a scheduled flight to Santiago-de-Chile on 15 January. On approaching Bermuda an engine failed and the onward flight was cancelled pending repairs. It was accordingly decided to transfer the *Star Lion*'s passengers and crew to the *Star Ariel*, while the *Star Ariel*'s passengers and crew would continue their journey to London aboard the *Star Lion* as soon as the engine trouble had been remedied. So it was that the *Star Ariel* was turned around at Bermuda.

The *Star Ariel* had a crew of seven and thirteen passengers. At 8.42 on the warm morning of 17 January 1949 the airliner lifted from the runway at Kindley Field and set course for the 1,100-nautical-mile flight to Palisadoes Aerodrome, Kingston, Jamaica. The flight was expected to take about five-and-a-half hours and the captain, J. C. McPhee, gave ETA as 2.10 that afternoon, listing Nassau and Havana as diversionary airports, but, with ten hours of fuel – a safety margin of four hours – and excellent weather, nobody really expected that it would be necessary to divert.

The first air-to-ground communication took place fifty minutes after take-off. *Star Ariel* reported to Kindley Field Airport Approach Control by radiotelephone that she was at 18,000 feet and changing to radio telegraphy to contact New York Oceanic Air Traffic Control.

As explained earlier, Bermuda is in the New York OATC area, but aircraft proceeding to or from Bermuda usually work with Station VRT, the Air Guard service operated on behalf of OATC New York by Cable and Wireless (West Indies) Ltd. At 9.35 the *Star Ariel* contacted VRT: 'I departed Kindley Field at 8.42. I am flying in good visibility at 18,000 feet. I flew over 150 miles south of Kindley Field [the boundary of Airport Approach Control where the aircraft changed radio frequency to contact VRT] at 9.32. My ETA at 30 degrees north is 9.37. Will you accept control?'

Thirty degrees north was the boundary of OATC New York. The usual procedure at such boundaries was to change radio frequency and contact the OATC area ahead, but on flights to Jamaica interference from other radio stations frequently made it impossible to establish contact with Kingston by day. It was therefore the accepted practice of aircraft on this route to work with either Nassau or New York or to re-establish contact with VRT until the 'plane reached the halfway stage in her flight when it should have been possible to contact Jamaica.

At 9.42 the *Star Ariel* reached thirty degrees north and announced that she was changing frequency to contact Kingston. The message was acknowledged by VRT, giving Captain McPhee complete clearance to change radio frequencies. At this point VRT and OACT ceased their Air Guard responsibilities.

The *Star Ariel* did not re-establish contact with VRT and the Flight Operations Officer assumed that the aircraft had either established communications with Kingston or was working with Nassau. At Kingston, where the Flight Operations Officer there had been notified of the *Star Ariel's* intention to establish contact, there was no word from the Tudor and it was assumed that the 'plane was working with Nassau.

At 11.27, two hours since take-off, the *Star Ariel* should have reached the halfway stage in her flight and the Flight Operations Officer at Kingston was awaiting word from the aircraft. Unfortunately radio conditions on the air-ground frequency were poor between 11.27 and 11.45; another BSAAC airliner, the *Star Panther* (the first Tudor to be built by A. V. Roe) could be heard vainly calling Nassau. The *Star Panther* called Kingston at 11.27 and asked them to contact Nassau on their behalf. Kingston tried at 11.39 but without success.

By midday Kingston was growing concerned about the *Star Ariel's* continued silence. The airliner's ETA was only a little over two hours away. The Flight Operations Officer waited until 1.10, an hour before ETA and then tried to contact the Tudor. There was no reply. Kingston then radioed the *Star Panther*, now only half an hour from Nassau, and asked her to try to raise the *Star Ariel*. The *Star Panther* made several attempts during the next eight minutes, but to no avail.

The *Star Panther* landed at Nassau at 1.43. There was still no word from the *Star Ariel*, now less than half an hour from ETA.

At 1.52 Kingston signalled Nassau requesting information about the *Star Ariel* and was told to stand by. After a few moments Nassau radioed that she had no information – the *Star Ariel* had not made contact with them!

At 2.10 the *Star Ariel* did not arrive at Kingston and there was still no word. VRT Bermuda contacted BSAAC and informed them that the *Star Ariel* had not made contact with any ground station for almost five hours and was now overdue. Two minutes later the USAAF base at Kindley Field requested information concerning the *Star Ariel* and at 2.54 BSAAC Operations Bermuda alerted all concerned that the *Star Ariel* was missing. Hardly five minutes was passing without somebody requesting information about the aircraft. At 3.05 an incident report was forwarded to the 215, 2nd Rescue Unit at Harmon AFB in Newfoundland. Further reports were sent to the 5th Rescue Squadron at McDill AFB at Tampa, Florida, and to the 1st Rescue Squadron at Ramey AFB, Puerto Rico, giving all the available information and asking that they take action as required.

The *Star Panther* left Nassau at 4.25, over two hours since the *Star Ariel*'s planned ETA, intending to dissect the Tudor IVB's track in a little less than three hours. Another search aircraft took off from Kindley Field, Bermuda, at 4.47 and flew along five hundred miles of the *Star Ariel*'s course, doing a ten-mile lattice search on the way back.

At 5.08 New York Air-Sea Rescue sent a message to the USAAF at Bermuda instructing an all-out search.

By 6.42 the *Star Ariel*'s fuel would have been exhausted. In the unlikely event that she was not already in the sea, she would have to ditch now.

The *Star Panther* reached 27 degrees north, 69 degrees west, at 7.05 and began to follow the *Star Ariel*'s route into

Bermuda, keeping watch for any wreckage and/or survivors. She arrived safely at Bermuda at 1.20 the next morning without having seen a trace of the missing 'plane.

The search for the *Star Ariel* was suspended during the hours of darkness, but rescue services used the time to organise a full search and rescue operation the next day.

In the early hours of Tuesday, 18 January 1949 BSAAC in London issued a statement to the effect that the *Star Ariel* was overdue on a flight from Bermuda to Jamaica and the Ministry for Civil Aviation announced that Major John Stokes, a representative of the Chief Inspector of accidents and the man who had conducted the preliminary inquiries into the loss of the *Star Tiger*, would leave for Bermuda later that day.

Meanwhile, a score of aircraft and numerous surface craft, including the aircraft carriers *Leyte* and *Kearsage*, the battleship *Missouri*, and six United States destroyers, had begun a widespread search along the *Star Ariel*'s route at dawn, and dozens of aircraft and ships joined the search throughout the day. By nightfall no trace of the airliner had been found. Search officials announced that the search would continue in a widening pattern for several days.

A special Board meeting of BSAAC was called on 19 January and it was decided to cancel all further flights of Tudor IV aircraft pending a detailed inquiry into the loss of the *Star Ariel* and an examination of each Tudor presently in operation. The Tudor IV scheduled to leave London on 20 January was accordingly cancelled and, in fact, no Tudor IV would ever again be used to carry passengers.

The search was resumed at dawn by more than twenty aircraft, but nothing was found by nightfall. Major Keith Cloe of the United States Air Force, who was in charge of the search operation, said that the hunt for the *Star Ariel* would be broadened to cover an area of 55,000 square miles south-west of Bermuda and would be continued until Saturday and even longer if debris were found. But nothing was found. More than a million miles were flown by search aircraft without a single shred of debris being found and the search was reluctantly abandoned.

An inquiry into the loss was held by the Chief Inspector of Accidents and his report was published on Wednesday,

21 December 1949. It was a slim document of fifteen pages and not as detailed as the report of the inquiry into the loss of the *Star Tiger*, but all the available information was carefully studied and much of the evidence which had been obtained during the inquiry into the loss of the *Star Tiger* was re-examined. The investigators failed to find an explanation for the loss. Every possible cause was examined and dismissed as improbable. The report concludes: 'Through lack of evidence due to no wreckage having been found the cause of the accident is unknown.'

Like *Star Tiger*, *Star Ariel* disappeared at the weakest stage in her flight, which is not without significance. There was no authorised and accepted procedure on the Bermuda–Jamaica route to guard against an aircraft signing off one radio frequency and not reporting to a new station. The *Star Ariel* evidently did not establish contact with a new station, but everyone thought that she must have done and this resulted in a long and possibly fatal delay before air-sea rescue stations were alerted. Whatever disaster overcame the *Star Ariel* it seems reasonable to suppose that it occurred shortly after 9.42 when she sent her final radio message, otherwise she would have established contact with another station. If this was the case she would have been down for fifteen hours or more before the search got underway at dawn on 18 January, by which time wreckage would have been dispersed beyond recognition.

However, delays do not account for the cause of the accident, which is in many ways far more mysterious than the disappearance of *Star Tiger*. Unlike *Star Tiger*, *Star Ariel* was flying at a good height, in excellent weather and in daylight, there were several alternative airports within reach and the 'plane carried over four hours' fuel for dealing with unexpected problems. The disappearance of the *Star Ariel* seems unfathomable and the explanation shall probably elude us forever.

The Tudor IV was withdrawn from service following the disappearance of the *Star Ariel* and was never used to carry passengers again, although the craft were used successfully and without accident on the Berlin Airlift. As for BSAAC, the Corporation soon ceased to operate and was absorbed by BOAC.

Sources

Chapters One and Two

Deakin, Michael and Willis, John: *Johnny Go Home* (London: Futura Books, 1976)

Fort, Charles: *Lo!* (New York: Claude Kendall, 1931; New York: Ace Books, n.d.)

Freeman, Dudley: '1975–The Year of Vanishing Wives' (London: *Sunday Express*, 19 October, 1975)

Hart, Penny: '7 Year Riddle of Lost Boy' (London: *Sunday Express*, 22 August, 1976)

Kane, Peter: 'Hitch-hike Killer Hunt' (London: *Daily Mirror*, 31 January, 1977)

Nationwide (BBC Television, 1 June, 1977)

Payne, Graham: 'Mummy Went Shopping . . . And Never Came Back' (London: *Weekend*, 16–22 July, 1975)

Payne, Joe: 'Has 128 Year Old Riddle Claimed a New Victim?' (London: *Sunday Express*, 22 February, 1976)

Sharpe, David: 'Mystery of the Blonde on Platform Two' (London: *Sunday Express*, 25 July, 1976)

Sunday Express London: 27 July, 1975; 14 March, 1976; 11 April, 1976; 23 May, 1976

The Times London: 5 August, 1873

Wilson, Colin: *A Casebook of Murder* (London: Leslie Frewin, 1969; London: Mayflower Books, 1971)

Chapter Three

Churchill, Allen: *They Never Came Back* (New York: Ace Books, 1960)

New York Times New York: 4, 6, 13, 16, 17, 24 December, 1946

Norman, Eric: *Weird Unsolved Mysteries* (New York: Award Books, 1969)

Chapter Four

Brennan, J H: *Beyond the Fourth Dimension* (London: Futura, 1975)

Edwards, Frank: *Stranger Than Science* (New York: Lyle Stuart, 1959; London: Pan Books, 1963)

Fort, Charles: *Lo!* (New York: Claude Kendall, 1931; New York: Ace Books, n.d.)

Keel, John A: *Our Haunted Planet* (London: Neville Spearman, 1971; London: Futura, 1975)

Norman, Eric: *Weird Unsolved Mysteries* (New York: Award Books, 1969)

Palmer, Stuart: 'How Lost Was My Father' (Illinois: Clark Publishing Co, (*Fate*) July, 1953)

Palmer, Stuart: letter dated 28 May, 1952 to Mr Webster of *Fate*

Payne, Herschel G: letter dated 17 March, 1977 to Robert Forrest

Rickard, Bob: 'Fortean Corrigenda: Disappearance of David Lang' based on research by Robert Forrest and Herschel G. Payne (London: *Fortean Times*, October 1976)

Shadewald, Robert: 'David Lang Vanishes – Forever' (Illinois: *Fate*, December 1977)

Steiger, Brad: *Strangers From The Skies* (London: Universal Tandem, 1966)

Chapter Five

(*indicates that the source gives Mr Reichardt's story of the First-Fourth Norfolk and the 'kidnapping cloud')

Aspinal-Oglander, Brig Gen C F: *Official History of the War, Military Operations, Gallipoli*, Vol II (London: *William Heinemann*, 1932)

Berlitz, Charles: *Without a Trace* (New York: Doubleday and Co, 1977; London: Souvenir Press, 1977)*

Blum, Ralph with Judy: *Beyond Earth: Man's Contact with UFOs* (New York: Bantam Books, 1972; Springfield, Mass: Phillips Publishing Co, 1974; London: Corgi Books, 1974)*

Brown, Raymond Lamont: *A Casebook of Military Mystery* (Cambridge: Patrick Stevens, 1974)

Carew, Tim: *The Royal Norfolk Regiment (The 9th Regiment of Foot)* (London: Hamish Hamilton, 1967)

Collyns, Robin: *Did Spacemen Colonise The Earth?* (London: Pelham Books, 1974; St Albans, Herts: Mayflower Books, 1975)

Edwards, Frank: *Stranger Than Science* (New York: Lyle Stuart, 1959; London: Pan Books, 1963)*

Edwards, Frank: *Strange World* (New York: Lyle Stuart, 1964; New York: Bantam Books, 1969)

Final Report of the Dardanelles Commission (London: His Majesty's Stationery Office, Cmd 371, 1917)

Flying Saucers (Amehurst, Wisconsin: Palmer Publications Inc, March 1968; Issue 46)*

James, Robert Rhodes: *Gallipoli* (London: B T Batsford, 1965; London: Pan Books, 1974)

Keel, John A: *Our Haunted Planet* (London: Neville Spearman, 1971; London: Futura Books, 1975)*

Nichols, Elizabeth: *The Devil's Sea* (New York: Award Books, 1975)*

Norman, Eric: *Weird Unsolved Mysteries* (New York: Award Books, 1969)

Pauwels, Louis and Bergier, Jacques: *The Morning Of The Magicians* (also published under the titles *Le Matin des Magiciens* and *The Dawn of Magic*) (Paris: Editions Gallimard, 1960; London: Anthony Gibbs and Phillips, 1963; London: Panther Books, 1963; New York: Stein and Day, 1963)

Steiger, Brad: *Strangers From The Skies* (London: Universal-Tandem, 1966)*

Steiger, Brad and Whritenour, Joan: *Flying Saucers Are Hostile* (London: Universal-Tandem, 1967)*

Times History Of The War, Vol II (London: *The Times*, 1916)

Trench, Brinsley Le Poer: *Mysterious Visitors* (Original title: *The Eternal Subject*) (London: Souvenir Press, 1973; revised edition, London: Pan Books, 1975)*

Vallee, Jacques: *Passport To Magonia* (Chicago: Henry Regnery Co, 1969; London: Neville Spearman, 1970; London: Tandem, 1975)*

Chapter Six

Many of these stories are recounted in the books about the Bermuda Triangle which I have listed elsewhere.

Brown, Raymond Lamont: *Phantoms, Legends, Customs And Superstitions Of The Sea* (London: Patrick Stephens, 1972)

Edwards, Frank: *Stranger Than Science* (New York: Lyle Stuart, 1959; London: Pan Books, 1963)

Fort, Charles: *Lo!* (New York: Claude Kendall, 1931; New York: Ace Books, n.d.)

Gould, Lt Commander Rupert T: *The Stargazer Talks* (London: Geoffrey Bles, 1943)

Miller, R De Witt: *Forgotten Mysteries* (Chicago: Cloud Inc, 1947)

Norman, Eric: *Weird Unsolved Mysteries* (New York: Award Books, 1969)

Potter, John S: *The Treasure Diver's Guide* (revised edition) (London: Robert Hale, 1975)

Sanderson Ivan T: *Invisible Residents* (New York: World Publishing Co, 1970; London: Universal-Tandem, 1974)

Schurmacher, Emile C: *More Strange Unsolved Mysteries* (New York: Paperback Library, 1969)

The Times London: 6 November, 1840

Villiers, Alan: *Of Ships And Men* (London: Newnes, 1962)

Chapter Seven

Berlitz, Charles: *The Bermuda Triangle* (Garden City, New York: Doubleday and Co, 1974; London: Souvenir Press, 1975)

Berlitz, Charles: *Without A Trace* (Garden City, New York: Doubleday and Co, 1977; London: Souvenir Press, 1977)

Charroux, Robert: *Lost Worlds* (original title *Le Livre des Mondes Oublies.* Published in the United States as *Forgotten Words*) (France: Editions Robert Laffont, 1971; New York: Walker Publishing Co, 1973; New York: Popular Library, 1974; London: Souvenir Press, 1973; London: Fontana, 1974)

Condon, Dr Edward U: *Scientific Study Of Unidentified Flying Objects* (otherwise known as the Condon Report) (New York: Bantam Books, 1969)

Edwards, Frank: *Stranger Than Science* (New York: Lyle Stuart, 1959; London: Pan Books, 1963)

Fort, Charles: *The Book Of The Damned* (Paris: Boni and Liveright, 1919; New York: Reinhart and Winston, 1941; London: Abacus (Sphere Books), 1973)

Gaddis, Vincent: *Invisible Horizons* (Philadelphia: Chilton Books, 1965; New York: Ace Books, 1973)

Glemser, Kurt: *Mysterious Disappearances* (Ontario, Canada: Galaxy Press)

Godwin, John: *This Baffling World* (New York: Hart Publishing Co, 1968; New York: Bantam Books, 1973)

Hoehling, A A: *They Sailed Into Oblivion* (New York: Ace Books, 1959)

Jeffrey, Adi-Kent Thomas: *The Bermuda Triangle* (New Hope, Pa, New Hope Publishing Co, 1973; New York: Warner Paperback Library, 1975; London: Star Books, 1975)

Jeffrey, Adi-Kent Thomas: *They Dared The Devil's Triangle* (London: Star Books, 1976)

Keel, John A: *UFOs: Operation Trojan Horse* (New York: G. P. Putnam, 1970; London: Souvenir Press, 1971; London: Abacus

Kusche, Lawrence David: *The Bermuda Triangle Mystery-Solved* (New York: Harper and Row, 1975; London: New English Library, 1975)

Landsburg, Alan and Sally: *In Search Of Ancient Mysteries* (New York: Bantam Books, 1974; London: Corgi Books, 1974)

Massey, Graham: *The Case Of The Bermuda Triangle* (London: BBC Television documentary, 16 February, 1976)

Massey, Graham: *The Case Of The Bermuda Triangle* (London: *The Listener*, 19 February, 1976)

Nichols, Elizabeth: *The Devil's Sea* (New York: Award Books, 1975)

Sanderson, Ivan T: *Invisible Residents* (New York: The World Publishing Co, 1970; New York: Avon, 1973; London: Universal-Tandem, 1974)
Spencer, John Wallace: *Limbo Of The Lost* (Westfield, Mass, Phillips, 1969; Revised and Expended Edition: New York: Bantam Books, 1973)
Spencer, John Wallace: *Limbo Of The Lost – Today* (Westfield, Mass, Phillips, n.d.; New York: Bantam Books, 1975)
Spencer, John Wallace: *No Earthly Explanation* (Westfield, Mass, Phillips, 1974; New York: Bantam Books, 1975)
Winer, Richard: *The Devil's Triangle* (New York: Bantam Books, 1974)
Winer, Richard: *The Devil's Triangle 2* (New York: Bantam Books, 1975)

Chapter Eight
The story of *Mary Celeste* has been told hundreds of times and is featured in many books about sea mysteries and almost every book about the Bermuda Triangle. The best source is said to be *Mary Celeste – The Odyssey Of An Abandoned Ship* by Charles Edey Fay and published by the Peabody Museum, Salem, Mass, in 1942. This book is difficult to obtain in Britain and readers may even find it impossible to obtain a copy through an inter-library loan scheme. However, Mr Fay wrote two consecutive articles about *Mary Celeste* for the magazine *Sea Breezes* in the 1950s and the relevant copies of this magazine might be available in larger public labraries. A very straightforward account of the mystery is contained in *The Bermuda Triangle Mystery Solved*, details of which are given below.

Bradford, Gershom: *The Secret Of Mary Celeste* (London: W Foulsham and Co, 1966)
Charroux, Robert: *Lost Worlds* (originally published as *Le Livre des Mondes Oubliés* in France by Editions Robert Laffont, 1971) (London: Souvenir Press, 1973; London: Fontana Books, 1974)
Fay, Charles Edey: 'The Greatest Sea Mystery' (Liverpool: *Sea Breezes*, n.d.)
Gaddis, Vincent: *Invisible Horizons* (Philadelphia: Chilton Books, 1965; New York: Ace Books)
Godwin, John: *This Baffling World No 2* (New York: Bantam Books, 1971)
Gould, Lt Commander Rupert T: *The Stargazer Talks* (London: Geoffrey Bles, 1943)
Hastings, Macdonald: *Mary Celeste* (London: Michael Joseph, 1972)
Hocking, Charles: 'Dictionary Of Disasters At Sea During The Age of Steam' (London: *Lloyd's Register of Shipping*, 1969)

Kolosimo, Peter: *Not Of This World* (London: Souvenir Press, 1970; London: Sphere Books, 1971)
Kusche, Lawrence David: *The Bermuda Triangle Mystery – Solved* (New York: Harper and Row, 1975; London: New English Library, 1975)
Lockhart, J G: *The Mary Celeste And Other Strange Tales Of The Sea* (London: Rupert Hart-Davis, 1965)
The Times London: 14 February; 28 March, 1973

Chapter Nine
Barker, Ralph: *Great Mysteries Of The Air* (London: Chatto and Windus, 1966; London: Pan Books, 1968)
Edwards, Frank: *Stranger Than Science* (New York: Lyle Stuart, 1959; London: Pan Books, 1963)
Fort, Charles: *Wild Talents* (New York: Ace Books, n.d.)
Gaddis, Vincent: *Invisible Horizons* (Philadelphia: Chilton Book Co, 1965; New York: Ace Books, n.d.)
Schurmacher, Emile C: *More Strange Unsolved Mysteries* (New York: Paperback Library, 1969)
Seattle *Post-Intelligencer* (Seattle: 22, 24, 26 August, 1947)

Chapter Ten
The story of Flight 19 can be found in almost every book and article about the Bermuda Triangle.

Begg, Paul G: 'Mr Berlitz – Again!' (Newfield, NY: *Pursuit*, No 42, Vol 11, Spring 1978)
Berlitz, Charles: *The Bermuda Triangle* (Garden City, New York: Doubleday and Co, 1974; London: Souvenir Press, 1975)
Berlitz, Charles: *Without A Trace* (Garden City, New York: Doubleday and Co, 1977; London: Souvenir Press, 1977)
Berlitz, Charles: 'An Observation on Critics Whose Appraisal of Phenomena Is Undisturbed by Personal Knowledge or Experience' (Newfield, NY: *Pursuit,* No 42, Vol 11, Spring 1978)
Board of Investigation into five missing TBM aircraft and one PBM aircraft convened by Naval Air Advanced Training Command, NAS Jacksonville, Florida, 7 December, 1945, and related correspondence. (Washington, DC: US Navy, 1946)
Edwards, Frank: *Stranger Than Science* (New York: Lyle Stuart, 1959; London: Pan Books, 1963)
Gaddis, Vincent: *Invisible Horizons* (Philadelphia: Chilton Book Co, 1965; New York: Ace Books)
Kusche, Lawrence David: *The Bermuda Triangle Mystery – Solved* (New York: Harper and Row; London: New English Library, 1975)

Landsburg, Alan and Sally: *In Search Of Ancient Mysteries* (New York: Bantam Books, 1974; London: Corgi Books, 1974)
McDonnell, Michael: 'Lost Patrol' (*Naval Aviation News*, June 1973)
Massey, Graham: *The Case Of The Bermuda Triangle* (London: BBC Television Documentary, 16 February, 1976)
Massey, Graham: 'The Case Of The Bermuda Triangle' (London: *The Listener*, 19 February, 1976)
Sanderson, Ivan T: *Invisible Residents* (New York: World Publishing Co, 1970; London: Universal-Tandem, 1974)
United States Navy: 'Fact Sheet' on Flight 19
Winer, Richard: *The Devil's Triangle* (New York: Bantam Books, 1974)

Chapter Eleven

The stories of the disappearance of the *Star Tiger* and the *Star Ariel* are told in almost every book about the Bermuda Triangle (listed elsewhere), but many of these versions are brief and suffer from erroneous information.

Star Dust

Report on the Accident to Lancastrian III G-AGWH which occurred on 2 August 1947 in the Andes Mountains, South America (London: His Majesty's Stationery Office, 1948)

Star Tiger

Barker, Ralph: *Great Mysteries of the Air* (London: Chatto & Windus, 1966; London: Pan Books, 1968)
Hyde, H Montgomery: *Strong For Service*, The Life of Lord Nathan of Churt (London: W H Allen, 1968)
Report of the Court investigation of the accident to the Tudor IV Aircraft 'Star Tiger' G-AHNP on 30 January, 1948, held under the Air Navigation (Investigation of Accidents) Regulations, 1922 (London: His Majesty's Stationery Office, 1948)
The Times London: 31 January, 1948; 2, 3, 4, 5, 17, 27 February, 1948; 23 March, 1948; 12, 13, 14, 15, 16, 17, 21 April, 1948; 15 May, 1948; 29 September, 1948

Star Ariel

Report of the loss of Tudor IVB "Star Ariel G-AGRE" which disappeared on a flight between Bermuda and Kingston (Jamaica) on 17 January, 1949 (London: His Majesty's Stationery Office, 1949)
The Times London: 18, 19, 20, 24 January, 1949; 21 December, 1949

Index